The Hidden Pathway

Herbert and Elsie Dawson circa 1939

THE HIDDEN PATHWAY

Compiled by
G.D.Buss

2000

Gospel Standard Trust Publications
12(b) Roundwood Lane
Harpenden
Herts
AL5 3DD
England

ISBN 1 897837 25 9

This edition first printed : 2000

Printed by
The Cromwell Press
Trowbridge

CONTENTS

ILLUSTRATIONS

FOREWORD

"In every mercy, full and free,
A sovereign God I wish to see;
To see how grace, free grace has reigned,
In every blessing He ordained.

Yes, dearest Lord, 'tis my desire
Thy wise appointments to admire;
And trace the footsteps of my God
Through every path in Zion's road."

The following pages eloquently echo and confirm the prayers of the good hymnwriter above. They relate the Lord's gracious dealings with one of His children, whom He prepared and fitted for the work of a pastor's wife, and the mother of a large family.

Elsie Dawson came from a generation of God's children who, clearly and unequivocally, were made willing to bear the reproach of Christ, and to put the things of God and His church before all else, whatever the cost. In our own generation, when the gold of real profession of the name of Jesus has become so dim, the following pages make us realize how shallow present day religion is, in general, from that which our forefathers were privileged to experience. "Chosen in the furnace of affliction", the gold of the Lord's dealings shine blessedly through the life and testimony of this dear child of God.

Her husband, Herbert Dawson, was the pastor of "Union" Chapel, Bethersden, Kent, for fifty-six years. His extensive labours and fruitful ministry, both in the pulpit and in his numerous letters, are still remembered by many older believers, with deep affection. The writings of his wife give a fascinating insight, behind the scenes, of a pastor's life. How true it is that, in God's account, not only those who go out to battle, as His servants do in preaching the everlasting gospel, receive their reward, but just as importantly, those that remain at home, and "tarrieth by the stuff," as David records, have their portion too, and are just as dear to the Great Head of the Church.

As one of the many grandchildren of the late Herbert and Elsie Dawson, it is a great privilege for me to append these few words to their writings. May a double portion of their spirit rest upon us each, who desire that the 'God of our fathers, be the God of their succeeding race.'

A section has been added from the writings of Herbert Dawson, giving his own call by grace, and to the ministry and pastorate at Bethersden. Also his own testimony to the worth of the godly wife, with which the Lord had favoured him, is included.

Sadly, there is no written record of the last thirty years of the life of Elsie Dawson. She continued as a loyal pastor's wife to the end, although her last years were years of great affliction. In August 1969, she passed peacefully into the presence of her Lord, whom she had been graciously enabled to serve for so long. The one enduring memory of her last days, to the writer of this foreword, is of her choice of hymn to be sung with the family on one occasion, just a few months before her end.

> "Peace by His cross has Jesus made;
> The church's everlasting Head
> O'er hell and sin hath victory won,
> And, with a shout, to glory gone."

This epitomized her hope and her religion. It was, also, the foundation of her life and her anchor in death.

G. D. Buss
October 2000

PREFACE

How very important and essential just ordinary things are. How much we realize this if, through some circumstances, we cannot enjoy them as formerly. How desirable then is the ordinary routine of life. Yet do we not at times, in our inmost mind, tend to despise that which, by its very regularity, is our common lot? But let us consider rightly God's greatest natural gifts to the world. How regularly, how consistently, daily, yearly, even through the ages since He first created them, have those gifts been bestowed upon sinful mankind dwelling upon the earth! The daily rising and setting of the sun at His appointed times: the moon also as it rules the night: His 'two faithful witnesses in the heavens': the stars also in their regular courses. There could be neither night nor day without these faithful witnesses. The seasons of the year. How regularly, noiselessly, and yet how effectively they come and go in the course of the year. There could be no growth, consequently no food, without them!

What mighty contrasts we can observe in God's creative work. Great mountains and little hills, mighty rivers and tiny rills, each bespeak the majesty of their Creator. The mightiest trees and the tiniest daisy upon our lawns are equally the work of His hands. The greatest and the smallest in the animal world, the tiniest bird in our garden and the fierce eagle nesting upon the highest crags on the mountainside, equally show forth the wonders of His almighty power. Yes, even the most minute of the insects, which, in the realms of nature, do the work given them to do, in destroying, by consuming, the impurities in the air we breathe. How wonderful, and yet how ordinary are all these things, and can we not say with one poet and rejoice to believe that:

"His hands the wheels of nature guide
With an unerring skill."

If, then, we can contemplate these things and rejoice in the manifest wisdom, power and love of God therein, how much more

9

should we do so as we contemplate His dealings toward us as His creatures, and especially so, since we can hope that, by His grace, we are His people!

Our lives may seem to be very ordinary ones. They may, at times, seem to be even monotonous, because of the sameness day by day. But take the things of which we have written. The sun, the moon and stars, the seasons, the rills and rivers, the mountains and hills, vegetable growth; the appointed work of all created things, the same now as at the beginning in their ordinary, everyday routine, yet grand because of this very sameness and regularity.

So let us view our ordinary lives. Sanctified by the grace of God, they too can become witnesses of God's faithful love and care. The very tiniest duty is as important, in its place, as the biggest one. The little child, learning its first lessons in tidiness and order by putting away its toys when done with, is making its contribution, remote though it may seem, to world order and peace. Let us thank God for all ordinary things: they are the gifts. In Him we live and move and have our being. May we strive therein to show forth His praise.

Elsie J.Dawson

HOPE THOU IN GOD

"Jesus Christ the same yesterday, and to day, and for ever."
Hebrews 13. 8.

Shall I forget the Almighty arm
  So often raised for my relief?
And view life's pathway with alarm,
  Falling a prey to unbelief.

And wilt thou slight, my soul, the love
  Which hitherto hath been thy stay?
And try by reason's power to move
  The mountains from life's rugged way.

Is that arm shortened? Dost thou fear
  Its power will insufficient prove?
Is God's ear heavy to thy prayer,
  Or changed to thee is Jesus' love?

No; no! my soul; though sins may cloud
  Faith's prospect, and have dimmed thy sight;
Thy God yet undertakes thy cause
  And still is leading thee aright.

What He hath been, He is, - will be
  For ever; for no change He knows:
The same today, as yesterday; -
  Then find in Him thy sure repose.

Elsie J. Dawson

PART I

ELSIE DAWSON (1890-1969)
BIRTHPLACE AND CHILDHOOD

Chapter 1

I was born at Wantage, in Berkshire, in the year 1890. My parents were both godly people and were themselves the offspring of godly parents, so that I was much more favoured than many of God's people have been in the influence that surrounded me from earliest childhood.

My parents were in humble circumstances, although, by the God-given wisdom bestowed upon them, we never knew the lack of any necessary thing. We were well (if plainly) fed and clothed and though my mother was always a most delicate person, she was a most careful and prudent manager in the home. We were from our early days taught to value the comforts we possessed and to take care of what we had. Our pleasures were very simple ones. Home was the centre of our world, and I think we knew more of real contentment than many children do now, although in these days they have many more toys and other facilities for amusement and recreation than we ever had. I was my mother's eighth child. Two sisters and two brothers older than I were living when I was born, but my parents had been bereaved in the years before my birth of a little boy of two years, a baby girl of five months, and another little one at birth. This was a very sad blow to my parents, and they often spoke about it when I was little.

My earliest recollection of all is that one Christmas Day, when I was about three years old, my father bent over a little bed where I was lying very ill, wrapped me in a blanket, and nursed me, saying as he did so, "that is better." It seems that I had measles with complications and had been unconscious for many hours; it was as I regained consciousness that my father took me up to nurse me. I recovered from that illness, but it left cardiac weakness from which I have suffered all my life. I had three

13

sisters and two brothers younger than I in the family, also one other little baby sister who died at eight weeks old. I remember that quite well, and have never forgotten my mother's grief at the bereavement. The ten children of my parents who survived were all spared until the youngest one of the family was fifty-five years old. The eldest, Mrs W. Hope of Abingdon, being the first to be taken from us. We lost our mother, Mrs. Aldworth, some years before my father was taken. She was sixty-nine years of age when she died and my father was eighty-three when he died. All of their sons and daughters were able to be present at the funeral of each, and, with the exception of one brother who could not reach my mother's deathbed in time, we were all present at the deathbed of each.

My father came of a very consumptive family (prone to Tuberculosis). His mother died when he was three years old and his father when he was fifteen. Father was the youngest of his father's family, and his eldest sister (Mrs. West) kept her father's house until she married William West (who later in life was made a minister and subsequently pastor of "Ebenezer" Chapel, Heathfield). His father then married an elderly lady with whom my father lived until her death, some time after his father's death. Soon after this he married my mother. She had been living as a children's nurse in London, and, during her stay there, she attended Mr. Gunn's chapel in Harrow Road. There it was that the Lord met with her, calling her by His grace under Mr. Gunn's ministry. A sister older than her was also living as a needlewoman in another situation there, and she too attended, and was greatly blessed under Mr. Gunn's ministry. She, as well as my mother, made a most sweet and triumphant entry into God's heavenly kingdom, when she came to her end at a good age. Their parents were godly people and they had a good hope of at least four of their family.

We children knew only one grandparent, my mother's father, Mr. Wellavise. Her mother died six months after Mother was married. Knowing that she was dying, and also that my father was a lonely orphan, (at that time living alone, as his stepmother was dead) she was desirous that my father and mother should be married before she herself died, so that she might see them settled in their home. She was greatly attached to my father. My mother has told me about her mother's death. For the whole of one night she was assaulted by the great enemy of souls, and feared she was deceived and would be eternally lost. Her godly husband and my mother and her sister were with her, and she told me that they could only pray and weep most of the night, witnessing her distress. Shortly before her death, the Lord appeared for her relief. Her mourning was turned into joy, and she triumphantly entered into her eternal rest. Her last words were, to her husband and daughters: "Go and -

  'tell to sinners round,
  What a dear Saviour I have found;
  I'll point to thy redeeming blood,
  And say, 'Behold the way to God.' "

My grandfather (who in his young days had been a soldier and was a Crimean War veteran) was wrought upon by the Spirit of God and called by His grace. He, by his lips and life, did strive to show forth the praises of Him who had thus brought him out of darkness into His marvellous light. He lived to be eighty-nine years of age. He was well-known and highly respected in our native town. He was a descendant of a Huguenot family who came to England in the days of persecution in France. When I read when young, the name "Valiant for Truth" in Pilgrim's Progress, I thought of my grandfather, as he was that indeed! He used to get into conversation with the young clergymen who were being trained under a ritualistic vicar at the high Church (Anglo-Catholic) in the town. He would point out to them the errors which they were imbibing in that system, and try, as enabled, to set forth the Truth of God in its simplicity and its grandeur. One of these young men very highly esteemed him and would often be in conversation with him. I have often wondered whether anything my grandfather said to him was owned of God for good to this young man.

In connection with these particulars of family relationships, this verse frequently comes to my mind:

> "Parents, native place, and time,
> All appointed were by Him."

And in my case, and that of my parents and grandparents, how right are the words of the Book:

> "One generation shall praise Thy works to another."

LINE UPON LINE – HERE A LITTLE – THERE A LITTLE

Chapter 2

I have often wondered whether I really have known what the new birth really is, and it has caused much heart-searching. I was, as a child, very timid and afraid. I was kept very tender in my conscience. Sin, even such sin as a very small child can comprehend, seemed to me a dreadful thing, and when I was far too small to express myself over these matters at all, I was conscious of a need of something or someone upon which or whom I could really rely. I could not define my feelings, for I was then only between four and five years of age. I went to school when I was very young (as children often did in those days) and as soon as I knew my letters, I began to try to read. (I cannot remember going to school for the first time, nor learning the alphabet) but I was only about five years of age, when one Sunday in Chapel, as I could not understand what the minister said, I thought I would try to read the hymnbook through. I thought if I could try to read one hymn at each service, I would soon know a lot of them. At that time, as my mother had a new baby and one other child younger than me with her, I sat with my father, who was singing leader, and consequently sat at a table in the corner of the chapel by the pulpit, with the deacons. Reading syllable by syllable, I went through the first hymn in Gadsby's Hymns, verse by verse until I read those lines:

"While Thy eternal thought moves on
Thy undisturbed affairs."

As I, with effort, read them, the meaning of them entered my heart. I recognised in them what I was longing for – something which was unmoveable, something which would remain – and I clung to them. They brought a feeling of peace and security. I was much too young then to understand my own needs and what would satisfy them, and much too shy, even if I could have expressed my feelings, to do so. But from time to time, since I have grown older and have looked back, the remembrance of that

17

incident in my earliest days comes back, or rather is brought back to my remembrance by the Holy Spirit, not only as a memory, but with a renewal of the sense of peace which they gave at first. I look upon that time as being the first indication I have of the Spirit's work within. The next memory I have, which abides with me, is that one Sunday when we came home from Chapel, the monthly magazines were put out on to the sitting-room table. As I noticed them, I thought, "Oh, I do want to be 'good' like Dadda and Mamma are, and like the other people who go to Chapel. If I read these books, like they do, perhaps I shall be too." So I tried hard to read some of it, but I could not make much headway with it. The next recollection I have of these things meaning anything to me was at day-school one day. We opened morning school by singing the hymn:

> "My heart and voice I raise
> To sing Messiah's praise.
> Messiah's praise let all repeat
> The universal Lord
> By whose Almighty Word
> Creation rose in form complete."

The next verse broke me down and tears came as I sang:

> "A servant's form He wore
> And in His body bore
> Our dreadful curse on Calvary!
> He like a victim stood
> And poured His sacred blood
> To set the guilty captive free."

But oh, what a sense of relief and lifting up I had when we sang the next verse:

> "But soon the Victor rose
> Triumphant o'er His foes
> And led the vanquished host in chains.
> He threw their empire down,
> His foes compelled to own
> O'er all the great Messiah reigns."

I never read that hymn (or part of it) or hear it quoted, but my mind goes back to that day in the classroom when it was made so real to me. I was then about six or seven years old. The next time I remember anything special, was when I attended a service in the chapel attached to our day-school. A man who was the clerk in the chief solicitor's office in the town, a very godly man, read, as the lesson for the service, in Isaiah chapter 28, verses 9-10. As he read: "precept must be upon precept; line upon line," etc., it at once came to my mind that God would teach me the Truth like that. As it was repeated again in the chapter it confirmed me. I was then about ten or eleven years old.

No one, of course, knew what was going on within me, and I was, like all others of Adam's race, a sinner, and I knew it! We were brought up all our lives under the sound of the Truth. Whenever possible, all of us were taken to the House of God regularly. I have clear memories of the preparations to get us each ready to start to walk to the chapel which was about one third of a mile distant. I can remember walking home with my father and hearing him talking of the "things of God" with the ministers, and I used to think that perhaps when I was old (as I childishly thought they all were) I might know these things like they did. The church in the town was a very ritualistic one. Also there was a large Anglican nunnery in the town too. Connected with the church, and this nunnery, were three large schools. One of these was a High School for Girls, one was equivalent to our modern County Grammar School, and the third was a kind of Industrial School and orphanage combined. Attached to the nunnery and in the same building was a penitential home. The nuns, or Sisters of Mercy, were the teachers at the different schools mentioned, and also supervised the women at the penitential home who, incidentally, did the laundry and all the other domestic duties connected with the nunnery and schools, so that Wantage was a very hot-bed of ritualism. We saw very much of some of the nuns, and also the priests who visited the nunnery. We children (of our family and other nonconformists) were forbidden to allow them to talk to us as we went to and from school. The nunnery was very close to our home, and so the same path to the town was used by them as by us.

We had a good nonconformist day-school in the town, which most, not all, Chapel children attended. The others, the national schools for girls and boys, were largely under the influence of the Church. Our schoolmaster was a godly man, an old-fashioned Methodist. He was very scholarly, and many who were trained at his school rose to high positions in various capacities. He lived to be a great age, and, in his retirement, lived very close to our Strict Baptist chapel at Grove, near Wantage, a time-honoured Cause of Truth, where he often went as a worshipper. He was regarded by the more modern Wesleyan Methodists as being out of date altogether! (He had been for many years a lay-preacher among them.) It was said contemptuously of him that he believed in the "old-fashioned Blood Theology." What an honour for him! What a condemnation for them! We were highly favoured as children with such an influence in our school life. We have often wished that the young people of today were thus favoured.

I lived quite close to the nunnery, as I have stated. One day when I was twelve or thirteen years of age, feeling oppressed because I felt to be so sinful, I was, all at once, tempted with the thought that, perhaps if I lived in a nunnery, shut away as they were, perhaps I could live a sinless life. I would state here that what troubled me just then was that I had listened to a sermon in which the minister spoke of separation from the world, and being made to hate the world and the things of it. I applied this term, 'the world', to God's creation all around, and I was not able to sort it out in my mind! I was then, and always have been, very fond of all the beautiful things in creation; trees, flowers, birds, and the beautiful aspects of the light and shade in the sunshine or cloud of a March or April day, and later, the beauty of the crops growing on the hills all around us. I did not think I could cease from admiring the beauty of them. I was not left again to desire to be a nun. Shortly afterwards, I was enlightened and encouraged by a hymn being given out at Chapel, and which was my prayer for a very long time, and it is so even now, sixty years later.

> "Save me, O God, my spirit cries,
> And on Thy faithful Word relies;"

Some few years later, I was wheeling an invalid in a Bath chair along the road which adjoined the one by the nunnery, when I saw on the side of the road a most beautiful little plant. It was a weed, but the beautiful formation of the leaves, their silvery colour, and the beautiful little yellow flowers which it bore, struck me, and almost immediately this came with power to me:

"And every labour of His hands,
Shows something worthy of a God."

As I went on, the next verse of the hymn flowed into my mind, and I was favoured with a sweet meditation upon it.

"But in the grace that rescued man,
His brightest form of glory shines;
Here on the cross 'tis fairest drawn,
In precious blood, and crimson lines."

I have looked back upon it with a warm heart many times since, and I have often found it very profitable when working in my garden, to think upon His name, who by His own almighty power created the earth and all that it contains. I was never again tempted to think that that was the 'world' to which the minister referred. I learned 'here a little and there a little.' "The whole world which lieth in wickedness" was a solemn reality, for I found I had by nature a heart that was in league with it. But I was, by grace, shown also that blessed Refuge and Hiding Place where sinners, such as I felt myself to be, could fly. "And a Man shall be as... a covert from the tempest;" "When the blast of the terrible ones *is* as a storm *against* the wall."

I would say to any Minister of the Gospel: "Remember, there may be in your congregation very young seekers, or those who are not familiar with our phraseology. So strive as you preach, to teach also." I lived an exceptionally sheltered life as a child and, when I thought over what the minister said, I was puzzled for the time being, and I feel that many are, unless some further explanation is given. From the age of 13½ to 17½ years I lived away from home. (Except for fourteen months in the London area, I was in my home town, but living with elderly ladies as companion help.) In these homes I met with others not of our own denomination. When visitors and others who came in knew of my attending a Strict Baptist chapel, I was, though so young, subjected to much unkind questioning. As I look back, I have been encouraged and surprised at how I was enabled, child though I was, to put to silence those who cavilled at the doctrine of election. One man said to me: "I suppose you people think that only you will be saved, like your father Philpot and father Gadsby." I was shocked by such talk but, as he said: "What do you people do with this?; 'Come unto Me', you read it ever so many times." Immediately this came to me, and I answered: "It does say, doesn't it? 'No man *CAN* come to Me, except the Father...draw him'? And it does say too: 'All that the Father giveth Me shall come to Me; and him that cometh to Me I will in no wise cast out.' " I was fourteen years old then. The man who taunted me was over sixty, but the Word of God silenced him. After that he would say hurtful things in front of me about 'our people.' He never asked me any more questions! He was the brother of the lady with whom I lived, and he lodged at her house. Though professedly a nonconformist he absented himself from all public worship, which thing, as a child, I could not understand, for I did not know of any of my relatives, who were all Strict Baptists, or our friends, who were not very regular in their attendance upon the means of grace and I thought that was the only right thing for anyone to do who was well in health, and able to do it.

While I was there, some missionaries came who were to open a mission hall in a village close to Wantage. I do not know to what denomination they belonged. The first day they were there (four of them) one of them said to me: "Are you saved?" I had never had anyone put that question to me before, and I was surprised that it was done. I answered quite truthfully: "I do not know." Another one said: "Well, you should know that! It is a thing you can be quite certain about." I said I was not certain at all. They began to say other things concerning it, when, all at once, it came to my mind to tell them that my father and mother and grandfather were all Strict Baptists, and that I attended that place of worship where my grandfather and my father were deacons. They said: "Oh!! Oh!" and from that time asked me no questions and said nothing more to me. I felt very glad that they did not. I was anxious even then that I should not build on a false foundation, and I did not understand their language concerning these things. I knew, by remarks they made to others, that they had no place in their hearts for those who belonged to our denomination. After being there for about sixteen months, my father and mother arranged for me to go to a situation in Ealing with my older sister. We were with Church people, who were very staunch to their profession, but they were tolerant, and respected our desire to go to a chapel, and always made it convenient for us to go, one at a time, to a service. We found a Strict Baptist chapel at Brentford, the nearest one to where we lived, though still quite a distance for us to go. The people there made us welcome, and some showed us kindness in making us welcome at their homes. That meant much to us as we were young and missed our homes and parents greatly. After a time, my father arranged for me to go to another place there in London, at Chiswick. My sister remaining in the other situation. (I was not really old enough for the first one.) The people with whom I now lived were Strict Baptists and attended Brentford chapel, but there I learned that not all Strict Baptists were quite like those among whom I had been brought up. 'Here a little and there a little, line upon line.' I was being taught knowledge. One day, the lady at whose house I was living came to me and said: "Elsie, are you saved?" I was quite taken back. I replied as I had done a year or more before, to the man who had asked me that question, "I do not know. I want to be." So she gave me a little booklet and said: "Well, I want you to read that." I believe it was entitled, *'Are You Saved?'* I did not understand the line of things in that booklet, and it certainly was of no help to me. She was a Strict Baptist by profession, but I think she was happier with others in other churches, in some ways. My health gave way and I had to return to my home. I was then about sixteen years old and, about that time, I had many little helps by the way. A lady who attended the chapel was desirous that I should go to live with her and her sister.

23

I was fond of the old people, and they seemed to be fond of me. The sister was not a Strict Baptist, although brought up as such. I used to hear her say: "I am not bigoted, you know." I used when I could do it, to go down to the chapel at Grove in the afternoon. The services there were morning and afternoon. At "Zion", Wantage, they were morning and evening. I had two or three helps there. Mr. Harris, the dear old deacon there, gave out one afternoon:

> "Water from salvation's wells
> Thirsty sinner, come and draw;"

I heard Mr. Emery preach from this text:

"The King's daughter is all glorious within:...She shall be brought unto the King in raiment of needlework: the virgins her companions that follow her shall be brought unto Thee."

Psalm 45. 13,14

As I listened, a hope sprang up that I was perhaps one of the 'companions that followed.'

I used to hear Mr. Emery, whenever I could, for this reason. He knew nothing about me. I thought, too, that he was a very stern and solemn preacher, and so I felt that if I did receive any encouragement under his ministry, I could look upon it as real. I was very anxious to have a real religion. That afternoon Mr. Harris, the deacon, gave out Gadsby's No. 956:

> "Christ has blessings to impart,
> Grace to save thee from thy fears;"

This helped me very much.

I kept these things hidden up as, I thought, and certainly never spoke of them to anyone. One Sunday evening, however, I was at my home and the organ was being played. I remember I began to sing a hymn which I had often read and used as a prayer, beginning:

> "Beset with snares on every hand,
> In life's uncertain path I stand;
> Saviour divine, diffuse Thy light,
> To guide my doubtful footsteps right."

As I stood by the organ singing it, I all at once noticed my mother watching me rather intently, and I had an intuition that she knew my secret, though she very wisely said nothing to me then. About this time, when taking the crippled lady out, I passed a shop with photographs and also small pictures in it. I did not stop but, as I passed, one small one caught my eye. It was that of a woman in deep waters, clinging to a rock or a cross. The title was *'Rock of Ages.'* It seemed just to portray what my feelings were. I never spoke of this until twenty or thirty years afterwards when I mentioned it to my husband, because I thought it was perhaps savouring of ritualism. But the influence it had upon my mind that day has remained for about fifty-five years. Again 'line upon line, precept upon precept.' I was seventeen then. I was taking the crippled lady, with her sister, to visit three cousins of theirs who lived in another part of the town. There were two ladies and their brother, whom they cared for, because he was mentally afflicted. These people were very strict Church people. Very kind indeed, and they were most friendly in their manner to me. I was exceedingly shy as a girl and had dreaded meeting these strangers (to me) and having tea with them. However, all was very pleasant. After tea they proposed a simple game of cards they had taught their brother (who was a little mentally retarded) to play this game. It needed an equal number of players, four or six. I felt very hard put to it. We had always been taught the evil of card playing, and forbidden by our parents to do it. I at first said: "I don't know how to play this," but the ladies said very kindly: "Oh, we can soon teach you, don't be nervous." I felt I had been cowardly, so I said: "I am afraid I cannot play, because my parents have told us we were never to play cards." I trembled very much as I said it and I felt very awkward because, as their guest, I felt I was perhaps rather rude to refuse. One of the ladies with whom I lived said: "Oh, this is quite harmless, Elsie. It can do you no harm at all." But to my surprise and pleasure, one of the ladies of the house said: "No, Elsie, you were quite right to say so. We wouldn't have you do what your parents forbid, for anything." Her sister agreed and one of them said, when I apologized for making it necessary for one of them not to be able to play, as she would have no partner, "Don't you mind at all. You are quite right to do what you are doing. I will gladly stay out of the game with you." They had a very lovely home. They were quite elderly and their home had been their parents'. She asked me if I liked old things. I said: "Yes, very much so. I have always been most interested in them and love to see them." "Well", she said, "You and I will have a lovely time together, for I am too." They had almost a museum of most lovely things; needlework of all kinds, some of the finest pieces made for infants were about three hundred years old. They had it packed in tissue paper, in a lovely old and very large bureau type of chest of drawers, which was itself very unusual. Then she showed me to another room; old silver, old china, some of it very quaint and lovely, old books and paintings most carefully treasured. We spent two hours or more looking at them all. When we went, she thanked me for the pleasure it had given her to show them to me, as I did appreciate their beauty and worth. I certainly had a most happy evening. I told them how I had enjoyed it. I mention this because other young people, as well as I, find it more difficult to make a stand for principle against those who are so friendly and so kind and whom you are very anxious not to hurt, than to make a stand when people are antagonistic in their manner. The precept and lesson learnt here was "Them that honour Me I will honour." I felt God had been good to me and had sheltered me even in that way.

One morning, not long after this, I was dusting the dining room before my ladies came in to breakfast. As I was by the big bay window, these lines of a hymn came oh so powerfully and sweetly to me:

"On such love, my soul, still ponder
Love so great, so rich, so free;
Say, whilst lost in holy wonder,
Why, O Lord, such love to me?"

I felt to be in a warm glow of love for a few minutes, then afterwards it was suggested to me that that could not possibly be for me, because I did not know enough about the things of God. I had heard in the ministry, and also by reading, of those who had been very deeply led into the terrors of the law, and then had had a very clear deliverance into gospel liberty and hope, and I had expected that I would have to learn in that way too. I have had to do so during my life since, in many ways, yet still as "here a little, *and* there a little." God is Sovereign in how He teaches His children knowledge – (I remember once in my life, when I was about forty, and we had to pass through (my husband and I together) a most trying time, when the Lord appeared and delivered us from it. One day this was spoken to me: "I have yet many things to say unto you, but ye cannot bear them now." It kept me very watchful and I often wondered in what providence the next 'Saying of the Lord' would be wrapped.)

I often seemed, to myself, to be a strange mixture of hope and fear, even though I wouldn't have changed my pathway with anyone. (This is a digression, but to go back to my youthful years.) About the same time as when those words came to me so sweetly, I had to go to the Post Office on an errand, and to get there, had to pass through our large Market Square. There was a Fair being held there and, of course, many people were gathered, and there was the usual noise and excitement. As I went along, thinking about the things of God which I was so anxious to know, I became so much aware of the terrible emptiness of it all that, meeting at that moment a woman who attended our chapel and was a member there, I said quite involuntarily to her: "Oh, what an empty sham it all is, isn't it? We do want something more than this." She looked very surprised at my saying this and just said: "Yes, it is." Afterwards I realized that I had never spoken to anyone about the things that I was exercised about, and I was not really very well acquainted with her, so she must have been surprised.

Going through the Market Place again a week or so later, I was thinking of our chapel and those I loved there, when this came quite powerfully to me: "We know that we have passed from death unto life, because we love the brethren." I inwardly said at once: "Oh, but that can't be enough. Of course I love them! They are all my friends, and ever so many are my own relatives." I was still thinking that I did not yet know enough to possibly be one who had passed from death unto life. But it came again and brought, for a little while, a sweet feeling of hope and love.

About this time, possibly before the last experience, I was in my bedroom one day and found that my heart seemed cold and indifferent and almost uninterested in the things of God. I felt alarmed, and tried to think about them and get rid of the coldness, but found I couldn't. Then I remember these lines coming to me:

"The rocks could feel Thy powerful death
And tremble, and asunder part;
O rend with Thy expiring breath,
The harder marble of my heart."

It was the language of my heart and I did pray for it to be done, for I feared I might be one who would be left out. It caused me much distress of mind but, looking back upon it, I could see that, even in this, the Lord was teaching me knowledge. A knowledge of the inward depravity of my heart and its utter indifference, by nature, to God and godliness. I wasn't left there long because, although I cannot remember that anything especially came to me, I realized the inward softening of the heart and that I was no longer indifferent, but instead, I was lively again in desire. It was indeed a fresh lesson. 'Here a little and there a little, line upon line, precept upon precept.'

Chapter 3

When I was about seventeen years of age, I entered upon one of the most outstanding experiences that I have known. Even now, fifty-five years afterwards, I cannot understand one or two things concerning it, though I know that one lesson I had to learn was, "Cease ye from man,...for wherein is he to be accounted of?"

My father, who had been suffering from a severe nervous breakdown and was recovering, was told, when he went to see the Managing Directors of the large engineering firm where he had been for some years Foreman of one section, that his services would no longer be required, as they were filling the places of the older men with younger ones from away. My father was then about fifty-one years of age and had worked there from the age of about sixteen. He had been very skilful in his work and had been highly esteemed by the late Managing Director who had died about a year before this.

It was a great blow to my father and he did not recover from the effect of this for some years. Our home life had been very happy. There was strict discipline, but also interest shown and encouragement given to us each in our youthful, lawful pleasures and aspirations.

My father seemed now, however, a different man in some ways. Looking back upon it now, fifty-six years afterwards, I can realize what the trouble was. My father was left for the time (and rather a long time) to a rebellious frame, and did indeed, (I fear) "dwell in a dry land," and I think that explains, in a measure, his attitude towards things that came to pass concerning myself.

He had been for years, deacon of the Church and singing leader and, after the opening of the Sunday school about five years earlier, he was made the superintendent. He was also, as I have stated, in a high position of responsibility at the works. He was very happy, diligent and interested in his varied responsibilities, so when he was suddenly deprived of them, there is no doubt he was left to murmur. He could get no suitable opening at Wantage, though he tried hard, as he didn't want to leave his native town or the chapel. However, in a very few months, he was moved in the providence of God to St Albans in Hertfordshire. A friend from the chapel, a member, had been moved there earlier. He had taken a fish business there. The shop and business next to his was for sale, and the property to let, so he wrote to my father concerning it. He went and saw it and decided it was the way for him to take, so he was moved in a very short while, after living in the house they left for about twenty-eight years. Naturally, I missed them and my house very much. I had never known another one. One of my married brothers still lived in Wantage, so that I had somewhere to go when I was off duty.

One day, when walking close by my old house, I met our

pastor and he said: "I don't like looking at these houses now. I never thought that Mr. Aldworth would ever leave us." He then said: "I suppose you will be going next." I replied: "Oh, I hope not. I did hope I should always live here and go to our chapel, and I did hope that perhaps, one day, when I am much older, I might even be a member, like my father and mother are." To my great surprise he said: "Well, Elsie, if you really feel like that, what is keeping you back now?" I replied: "Oh, I am not nearly fit or good enough for that. I only hoped perhaps that one day I might be, for I do want to be amongst God's people." He replied: "Well, all I shall say to you is this. If you wait until you feel you are fit, you will never do it. And remember, all the fitness God requires us to feel is our need of Him!" With that he left me. But from then on an exercise was commenced in my heart concerning it. I could not get away from it, night or day, nor did I want to. To me it seemed to be one of the greatest privileges with which anyone could be favoured, to be permitted to follow the Lord Jesus in His ordinances, but the great question was – Was I the right character to go through it? It was so great a thing that I wanted a sure word on which I could go forward. I said nothing to anyone at all, at the time, about it, but sought every opportunity to be alone, to seek the mind of the Holy Spirit concerning it. One morning I had to go into the town on an errand for my ladies, which gave me a quiet little walk first, before reaching the shops. The weight of the exercise of mind was very pressing upon me, when all at once I found myself to be almost overwhelmed by a sense of the love of God, so shed abroad in my heart as to lift me above everything surrounding me. For a few short moments I felt to be in His embrace. I could never describe the happiness I felt in that short time. Then this came to me so powerfully, "Suffer it to be so now: for thus it becometh us to fulfil all righteousness," and I knew that I could venture forward. But I wanted it confirmed and again the word came to me with even greater power. When I next saw our pastor, I told him that I must venture forward, but oh, I did dread the Church Meeting, as I did wonder what I could say to them. I wrote to my parents, but oh how disappointed I was when my father replied. I found that he was against me going forward in it, being sure, he said, that the pastor had taken advantage of their absence to persuade me into it. I wrote back to him, but nothing moved him from that obsession. Meanwhile the Church Meeting was arranged and I, and one other, went before the Church. I was very timid (I was then seventeen years old) but as I started to speak, this came so sweetly to me, "Plenteous grace with Christ is found, grace to pardon all my sin." I quoted it to them and spoke of it as being all my hope and desire. I did feel to hang upon it for time and eternity. After the Church Meeting, the deacon and several members spoke to me so kindly and encouragingly. They had been unanimous in their vote for me to be received as a candidate for baptism. It was all so wonderful to me that I should be so favoured in that they should receive me as one with them, that I was filled with wonder and joy. The desire which had been so great within me during my childhood up to that time, seemed to be about to be fulfilled, but, I was about to be put to a very crucial test. My father still persisted in his attitude against it. He had written to the pastor (though I was unaware of it) protesting against it. One day, our pastor's wife said to me: "I think you must have written home very differently to what you told us for Mr. Aldworth to have written to Mr. Clack as he has done." I was greatly distressed by it, and couldn't understand it at all. (I was not then aware that my father had already begun to turn in his feelings toward the pastor, before he left Wantage, because of some things in which they differed. Being quite ignorant of this, and only knowing of the time when they had been great friends, I was perplexed and distressed.) I assured Mrs. Clack that I had written as I had spoken, but I was wounded greatly, for I knew, in my heart, it had all been so real to me. The exercises night and day, and then the joy and grace I had experienced in going before the Church. It seemed such a sad climax; and from so unexpected a quarter. Arrangements went on for the Baptizing Service, as I still felt I must go. My father had forbidden it, both as my parent and as a deacon of the Church, but I still clung to the word, "Suffer it to be so now." I said to Mrs. Clack one day: "If my father was an ungodly man, I should know that he would be opposed, but should also know what to do. But I know he is a godly man, and it seems so difficult to know what is right to do, because I have always felt it was wrong to disobey him, for it does say, 'Children, obey your parents in the Lord'." One elderly, lady member, said to me also one day: "Look to the Lord with steadfast eye, And fight with hell by faith." I had never spoken to anyone but the pastor and his wife about the opposition, but I expect they had mentioned it to her. Even then, I could not see nor understand that, to go against my father, as he was a godly man, would or could be 'fighting with hell', as I would have done, had he been ungodly. I was indeed in a strait. (I have realized since, but I did not know it then, that even a godly man can be left to be in a very wrong frame of mind.)

The Baptizing Service had been arranged for a Thursday evening, and I had made the necessary preparation for it, when on the Wednesday evening, my brother called at the house where I lived. He asked me if I still thought of going forward to be baptized. I said: "Yes". (I had not discussed it with him at all, because he was not then a Church Member, nor was his wife, though I am sure they both were godly people.) "Well", he said: "don't you think it would be better to wait?" I said I didn't know. He said: " 'Gold in the furnace tried Ne'er loses aught but dross'. Waiting would be like trying it." Then he went on: "Well, I have called here because I have had a telegram from Dad to say that, if you go forward, he will come down tomorrow and publicly forbid it at the service time."

Here indeed was a test, and alas, to my sorrow, I failed. How many times I have felt since, oh, if only I had obeyed the heavenly vision, and put the earthly command on one side. The Lord would have made His way straight before me. His command was: "Suffer it to be so now:." A greater one by far than my father's that I was to wait. But I yielded and said I would wait, and my brother sent a telegram to my father to that effect. My brother saw the pastor to tell him, for I was much too distressed and upset to do so myself. There was one other candidate, and I had quite intended to go to the service to witness it, but the pastor sent a note to my ladies asking them not to let me go out that evening, as he would find it too trying to have me present. I had hoped to get some comfort and light by going, but when they told me that they should not let me go out, I felt forsaken indeed.

I went into my bedroom and I knelt down, but I could not pray. I heard the chapel friends, the pastor, his wife and daughter, and others who lived close, going by to Chapel, but I felt as though a big black curtain had fallen over me, and I was desolate. I had no access to prayer, no sweet communion with God, with which I had lately been favoured. And yet, in my heart, I knew that I had truly desired to do what was right. It was hard travelling. It is a bad thing to cast away our confidence, but I did not know then that I had done so. I did it ignorantly then, because I had no one near to make it plain to me. I thought it was my duty to obey my father, and I couldn't make it all lay straight. How many times since then have I had to pray:

"Make Thy way plain before my feet,
My God, be Thou my Guide."

When I first met the pastor after this, he said to me: "There must be something that your father knows about you, Elsie, that made him oppose your baptism. He has nothing against me." That remark from him wounded me greatly. It did hurt. "The spirit of a man will sustain his infirmity; but a wounded spirit who can bear?" I became quite poorly and weak physically, but my ladies (though they said nothing to me concerning it, for they neither of them had been baptized) were quietly sympathetic which, as I lived with them as a companion help and so was with them all the time, was very kind and un-embarrassing. I appreciated it greatly, because the pastor and his wife and others (with the exception of the godly old deacon) were very cold to me at the chapel. Although I did not realize it until long afterwards, it was my first experience of fellowship with the Lord Jesus Christ in His sufferings. For we read: "And *one* shall say unto Him, What are these wounds in Thine hands? Then He shall answer, *Those* with which I was wounded *in* the house of My friends."

33

I had indeed been wounded by those I loved best, concerning those things which were more to me than anything else in life. But I have realized since, that I have often prayed that I might know Him and the power of His resurrection. Since then, in my life, I have had to have further fellowship with Him in His sufferings, but, I bless God that I have, too, had some sweet experience of the "power of His resurrection." We shall never, in this life, fully apprehend the greatness and magnitude of that power. "Behold, I make all things new." That was the experience I was to be favoured to enter into, some three years later, but for the time being I was in a bewildered condition. I seemed to be 'cut off from my part.' I did not now know where I was in divine things. I seemed dark, and afar off from light and warmth and life. Like one in a dark dungeon, yet longing acutely for liberty. I had to go on in that state for a very long time. I often went down to Grove chapel in the afternoon, and sometimes I did seem to have just a little help, but soon returned to my own sad state. Shortly after this, I had a letter from my father to ask me to give in my notice to the elderly ladies with whom I lived, because my mother was in a sad state of health, and I was needed at home. My ladies were very sad about me leaving them, and I was sorry for their sakes, but I was very fond of my parents; my mother in particular. She was frequently ill, in fact, never really well in health, but very persevering in doing all she could in her home life for her husband and children, whilst being very retiring in her manner to those outside her home. She was a truly godly woman. I was seventeen and a half when I went home to them, and I stayed with them until I married at twenty-five years of age. The first two years at St Albans were dark days indeed. My father was still under a cloud, and grieved much over his separation from his activities in the Cause of Truth at Wantage. He was far from well in health, as he had not yet fully recovered from the breakdown which had led up to this change in his life. Mother was in a very poor state of health, and we often feared that she would not recover. This grieved her, as she was very desirous to keep my father in the business, as she knew how poorly he really was. She, too, missed her relatives and the chapel friends at Wantage. Her deafness made it difficult to quickly make an acquaintance with people who were strangers. I had two brothers and a sister who were still quite small children at school. The business life was quite fresh to me, but I quickly became very interested in it. It was situated in a newly developed part of St. Albans, and consequently needed careful application to it for it to be built up and really support us as a family. My father was given the wisdom needed, and the caution and prudence to keep free from debt, God blessed the labours of his hands, so that gradually, a sound business was built up. At first it was a hard struggle. I have often stood in the shop and prayed that customers might come in to buy. As in every other lawful calling in life, God's people have to realize increasingly their dependence upon Him for all; whether temporally or spiritually. At first we were not happy or at home in the chapel there. The ministry of the man who was then the pastor, was not what we were used to and did not contain the 'certain sound,' which it should do. We went from place to place, at least, my father did. Occasionally he hired a conveyance, and we went to Welwyn, where one or two of the ministers whom we knew and whose ministry we loved, preached. Owing to my mother's ill health, and also having three young children whose ages ranged from eight to twelve years, it was not possible to do this often (there were not motors then available, only an open, horse conveyance). After some time, my father and other people who were equally unhappy at the local chapel, drew up a letter to the deacons there, to ask them if it would not be possible to have a sounder line of preaching in their pulpit, so that they could regularly attend and support the Cause to the utmost of their ability. In due time this was attended to, and, as a family, we were able to attend regularly. The children went to the Sunday School and I to the Bible Class. In this class I was, from time to time during the six years I was attending it, blessed under the ministry of Mr. George Whitbread, who conducted it. We had been at St Albans nearly two years before I knew of the Class. My father had not been willing for us to attend the chapel under the ministry of their pastor. A sister of mine, who was in domestic service, had lately taken a situation in St. Albans, and as she did not live at home, did not feel that she had to obey my father, re attending the chapel. She heard of the Bible Class and told me of it and persuaded me to go with her. My mother felt that I ought to be allowed to be free in this matter. This was very shortly before the alteration in the ministry when we could all attend, which we did, and oh, what a difference it made to once more be regularly attending the House of God, as we had always before been wont to do. About three years previously, Mr. Whitbread had been called by grace in a very marked manner, when on his police duty at the Town Hall. He had heard the Scripture being read in one room of the Hall, while he was in the corridor on duty, because of a very large meeting of a political nature being held in the larger part of the building. That scripture was used by God to arrest him as a sinner before a holy God. He began to search the Scriptures (when he could do it (as he thought) unnoticed in his home). His godly wife, however, had keen eyes. She had long been praying that he might be called by grace, and was given a promise that he would be. He was kind as a husband and father, and was a morally upright man, but would have nothing to do whatever with religion, though he did not oppose his wife or children going to Chapel. His wife was under increasing exercise of mind and felt she could not give up her request. One day there were Special Services (afternoon and evening) at the chapel. She wanted to go, but her store of housekeeping money had been used, and she did not like to go with nothing for the collection. She got ready, but the time for the service came and, though she had prayed that she might have something provided, she still had nothing for the collection. She was weeping under disappointment and also because of the burden laid upon her heart concerning her husband's spiritual state, as she went down to the coal cellar to get coal for her fire. Then she saw something shining below the grating where the daylight came in for the cellar. It was a half crown (12½p) piece. (The cellar grating was in the pavement of the street in which they lived, and it had been dropped by someone passing and had rolled onto the top of the coal.) She picked it up, got ready, and went to the chapel (late as she was) still under great stress of mind, and as she walked to her seat, the minister announced his text: "Thy prayer is heard." This was applied with power to her, and she felt that her many prayers had been heard, and, God was about to grant her a gracious answer of peace. It was very shortly after this event (which she herself told my parents and I, when she was visiting us and had tea with us in our home) that she had the great pleasure of seeing her husband searching the Scriptures and afterwards, on one Sunday evening, asking her if he might come to Chapel with her and their children. The Spirit of God worked mightily in him. He was brought out and made manifest as an heir of grace. He joined the Church very shortly afterwards. He became very much exercised concerning the ministry, and was later sent out by the Church, though he received bitter opposition from some therein. As a member, he was instrumental in obtaining a different line of ministry in the chapel.

Meanwhile, as I was from time to time helped with a little help, I became deeply exercised again about baptism. But I was so afraid that it was not right for me to think of it. I did not know where I was as regards the things of God. When I drew back at Wantage, a dark cloud came upon me, and I very seldom was able to rise above it. One day I went to the Bible Class, feeling, oh, so shut off and desolate, wondering if I ever had really known the joy and peace, which I did think I had been favoured with when I first went forward to join the Church. Truly I felt I was 'cut off from my parts.' When I got to the Class, Mr. Whitbread's subject was Ezekiel's vision of the dry bones. Under that address, I felt myself raised to a hope that the Lord would again appear and raise me up, and 'breathe upon me (slain as I felt to be) that I might live.' From that time, here a little and there a little, I was led on and raised again to a comfortable hope.

Chapter 4

I led an exceedingly busy life, seldom having any spare time, as even then my father was in poor health, but very bravely doing all he could to keep the business well attended to. He was a very industrious man and, as he came out of the cloud of depression, which his severe nervous breakdown had caused, he became like he had been in former days, genial and kind, but it was found that his heart had been badly affected and weakened by his illness, so that he could not work as he had done before. I used to try, when I went to my bedroom to change my dress just after dinner, to get a little spare time just to read a few verses of the Scriptures, and also to try to pray. One day, I opened the Bible and read this: "And therefore will the LORD wait, that He may be gracious unto you, and therefore will He be exalted, that He may have mercy upon you: for the LORD *is* a God of judgment: blessed *are* all they that wait for Him." Oh, that was meat to eat indeed. It seemed to stand out on the page for me. As I went on to my work in the shop again, I thought: 'A waiting Saviour, waiting to be gracious! A waiting sinner, waiting to be blessed! Oh, we must come together soon.' Oh it was a "word in season," "*like* apples of gold in pictures of silver."

Another time in my room I well remember, I was feeling so tempted that I should, even if I possessed any religion at all, outlive it, for it seemed so small and so obscure. I remember thinking, if I lived to be three score years and ten, it would never, never last all that while. (I was not, or only just, twenty then.) This came very powerfully to me: "Who are kept by the power of God through faith unto salvation ready to be revealed in the last time." That again was indeed a "word in season." Another time, I felt robbed and spoiled of all spirituality of mind, by having to interview the travellers and do the buying for the shop, to relieve my father who was poorly. When I could get to my room (as I was used to doing) I knelt down to pray. I found, to my great distress that I could not utter one word. I got up from my knees, feeling most distressed. I felt that, if I couldn't even pray, I must be far off indeed. As I was going out of my room to go back into the shop, this came so powerfully and gave me the help I required. "Pray, if thou canst or canst not speak; but pray with faith in Jesus' name."

On each of these occasions, I found that, at the Bible Class the next Sunday, Mr. Whitbread was led to speak of these experiences. The procedure in Bible Class was for him to choose a chapter for us to read, and then to comment on the chapter, or one or two verses of it. On the occasion of the first one, it came to my turn to read, "Therefore will the LORD wait," etc. It was a wonderful confirmation, and I know I found it difficult to read it because it touched me so. On the third occasion, after speaking on the subject of prayer and what true prayer was, Mr. Whitbread closed his address with this: "Pray, if thou canst or canst not speak; but pray with faith in Jesus' name." These 'little helps' were so good to me, as I had feared, in my darkest days, that I should never again have a 'token for good.' Here was another line of teaching, again 'line upon line,' and that was to experience this; that God never does, nor ever will, forsake the work of His grace which He has begun in the heart of any sinner, be they young or old!

Then I became tempted by this. Mr. Whitbread took the Bible Class, but was not invited to preach at St. Albans, even though the Church had sanctioned him going into the ministry. He went to two or three Causes around on Sunday evenings but, up to that time, I had never heard him preach. So it was presented to my mind that, if he was not a truly God-sent minister, then those little helps in the Bible Class would not really be of God. This greatly distressed me, but I did not say anything to anyone at all, either about the helps I had, or the temptation I had concerning them. Just at this time, Mrs. Whitbread gave me and one or two others, an invitation to have tea at their house, after Bible Class. Mr. Whitbread took us by a longer but quieter walk from the chapel to their house and on that occasion, while his daughter was talking to the other friends, Mr. Whitbread walked beside me because, he said, he had it upon his mind to tell me how he was called into the ministry. He hoped that if the Lord used him to be a help to anyone in the Bible Class, he felt that he would like them to know that he was not going 'a warfare at his own charges.' Oh, how that relieved my mind, and broke the power of the temptation. Once again I proved Satan to be a liar. As I felt to be again restored to a hope that I was among the people of God, I again became very much exercised concerning baptism. It stayed with me night and day. I often asked that the supplying ministers (who knew nothing of my exercises or of me) might be led to speak of it and, from time to time, they did. One Sunday evening after the service, my father and mother and Mr. and Mrs. Whitbread, walked home together with my sister and myself. We were talking about the service which we had just come from, and which we had each found to be encouraging and helpful. As Mr. Whitbread shook hands with me, a little apart from the others, he said: "And how did you feel about the service tonight, Elsie?" I answered exactly as I felt just then: 'This people shall be my people, and their God my God.' To my great surprise, I received a letter from him two days afterwards, telling me what a great encouragement and help it had been to him that I had answered as I did. He said that for months he had prayed that the Lord would work amongst us at the chapel and manifest His Power, by causing some to feel constrained to confess Him in this way. As no one had ever written to me like that before, I did feel greatly softened, humbled, and yet encouraged. Shortly afterwards, I had to go away from home to keep house for my sister who had had her first baby, and was rather poorly. While I was there, and rather lonely, I had a favoured time in my own soul. The former days, before I had drawn back from baptism, were brought back to my remembrance. The former hopes and evidences and helps which, while I was in the dark, desolate state, had been hidden and obscured. Now new light shone upon them and I could rejoice in them once more. While there, I wrote to my friends Mr. and Mrs. Whitbread, and told them a little of my exercises and helps, hopes and desires. The first Sunday after I came back, Mr. Emery was preaching at St. Albans. He, of course, knew nothing of my exercises but, had he known that morning what I had written to my friends, he could not have gone into them more. Mrs. Whitbread and I were first out of Chapel, and she said to me: "Oh, Elsie, what more do you want than this? If that man had seen the letter which you sent us, he couldn't have gone into your case more. It was almost as though he was giving the answer to you!" It was our turn to entertain the minister to dinner and tea. As Mr. Emery was an old friend of my parents, and had baptized my eldest sister (Mrs. Hope) at Richmond many years before, they were very pleased to have him. For my part, I had made up my mind that, beyond what ordinary courtesy demanded, I would say nothing to him. I was inwardly praying that, if the encouragement that I had had in the morning was really of the Lord, Mr. Emery would be led to speak of baptism in such a way that I should know that it was right for me to seek to walk in His ordinance.

He took a text in the morning in which he alluded to it (the ordinance), because he said that he felt solemnly persuaded that someone was listening that morning who was concerned about it. In the evening he went to within five minutes of the close of his sermon, when he said: "I am persuaded that someone is listening to me who is exercised about the ordinance, and I am compelled to turn aside from my subject and speak about it," which he did in a very feeling way. I said nothing about it to anyone then, but the following Sunday a Church Meeting (quarterly one) was announced for the following Friday evening. The minister who was preaching that Sunday (I believe it was Mr. Evans who was at that time pastor of "Rehoboth", Tunbridge Wells.) had spoken so sweetly of the love of God, and I felt such love to Him and His people and His ways that, after hearing the Church Meeting announced, as I went down the aisle to go out, I spoke to Mr. Whitbread and asked him to bring forward my name, as I did desire to be baptized. Quite unknown to me, a younger sister of mine did the same thing. She knew nothing of my exercises, nor I of hers, but we were constrained to do this, under the same sermon.

After I had done this I felt, for a time, more happy than I can describe, feeling that I was restored. After a day or two, however, I began to realize, that as my father and mother had some time before transferred their membership to St. Albans, they would be there when my name was brought forward. (I did not know then about my sister's name being brought forward too.) I did not feel that it would be kind to them to let them go to the Church Meeting ignorant of it, and yet, after my previous experience, I shrank from mentioning it to my father, for fear he should again oppose. I had nothing more to say than I had said before, and I thought perhaps that was not enough. Yet I felt I could not possibly go through all that anguish of mind again. It was the week when I usually went to London to the warehouses to buy things in the drapery line, which had been ordered, and also to stock up again in the shop. I went every fourth week and, this particular time my father was going too, as he wished to see some things he required from there. Usually I went alone. I had said nothing to them, but I thought: "Well, we have a long walk to the station, we shall have the train ride, and also we shall be coming back. I shall tell him then." After the business was finished in the warehouse, we went into Bunhill Fields (which I often did until it was time for my train home). We met Mr. Light there, and my father and he entered into conversation. Afterwards my father said he should like to go to "Gower Street" Chapel (The old one it was then). We had some tea, I believe in a restaurant, instead of going back home. Mr. Edward Carr of Bath was preaching that evening. I did not know him nor had I ever heard him preach. I went into the chapel, tempted, tossed, and harassed in my mind. I had not told my father about the Church Meeting and what he would hear there. I began to fear it was all a mistake, and I wished I could just go away where no one knew me. But, as we sat down in the chapel (we had trouble in finding it and were a little late going in) they were singing the hymn, "What cheering words are these." When we came to the verse:

"'Tis well when joys arise;
'Tis well when sorrows flow;
'Tis well when darkness veils the skies,
And strong temptations blow."

I was helped and encouraged to feel I was being led aright and that, in spite of all my fears, I was a right character to go forward in the path of obedience. I then thought: "Well, Mr. Carr is a complete stranger to me. He knows nothing about me or my exercises. If he should be led to speak of baptism, I shall <u>know for certain</u> that it is right for me to do this thing." Oh, how eagerly I listened, when he announced his text and, as he preached, how I longed for him to mention it, but it came to the very end and my heart sank, when he said: "Well, there is someone here perhaps who is saying: (his text was, "Seek the Lord, and His strength: seek His face evermore.") 'Well, I have sought Him in all the ways of which you have spoken and yet I have not found Him'. Well, there are yet two more ways in which you may seek Him. One is baptism and the other is the Lord's Table. Seek Him there. You <u>shall</u> find Him. Amen!" I was like someone set free, and I went out of the chapel and to the station to go back home with my father, really rejoicing in hope. When we were walking from the Midland Station to my home, I said to my father: "I expect you will be going to the Church Meeting, won't you?" He said: "Yes, if all is well. Why?" I said: "Well, you may be surprised, but you will hear my name mentioned, and I didn't feel it was kind to you and Mother for me not to tell you beforehand." He said: "Well, I am glad to know it and I am <u>not</u> surprised, for your mother and I have watched you and we have expected it." Oh, how glad I was. I was favoured for quite a time to walk in the light, and to rejoice in the Lord and in the power of His might.

Mr. Whitbread was not then a deacon of the Church, but he said at the Church Meeting (I was told afterwards) that he thought there should be a Special Church Meeting to hear the testimonies of the candidates, but the old deacon, who acted as senior deacon, would not consent to anything more than the normal quarterly one, which meant we had to wait three months before going before the Church.

This was a time of hopes and fears, but, for the most part, I was kept quiet in my mind, though I did feel that the warmth of love that I had felt seemed, at times, to abate, whilst it never went right out. I had to learn, here a little, there a little, that Jesus was the Saviour, however much I changed, and that my feelings were not for me to rest upon or in. Round about this time, Mr. Evans was preaching at the chapel. I do not remember his text or anything else about the service, but in prayer he just quoted: "This same Jesus." The words fastened upon me and I upon the words, and the sweetness of it remained for a long time, and even as I write, fifty years after, I can still recall how good they were to me. Mr. Whitbread and one other, who was a deacon at the chapel, were appointed to visit me previously to the next Church Meeting, quite a long while before. On the morning of the day they were coming I was busy helping my mother by lighting the copper clothes boiler fire for her. As I was busy I thought: "Oh, what shall I tell them this afternoon when they come? I have no outstanding beginning or big things I can speak about, like some have."

Immediately, this Scripture flowed into my heart: "The Spirit of God moved upon the face of the waters." Immediately, I could see how He, by His Spirit, had moved upon my heart as upon the waters, giving life in desires and longings for Him even in my very early childhood, and though then almost unrecognisable as such. His Spirit had wrought a new creation within me! That text has been a great comfort to me, and a sure evidence given to me then which Satan, though he has often tried, has been unable to take away from me. When the Church Meeting was held, I was not able to say much before them, but I remember finishing what I said by these lines:

> "My hope is built on nothing less
> Than Jesus' blood and righteousness;
> I dare not trust the sweetest frame,
> But wholly lean on Jesus'name."

I would have felt it was presumption to have dared to use the last two lines of the verse, (i.e. "On Christ the solid Rock I stand; All other ground is sinking sand.") nor did I even think of them then, but those I quoted were the real language of my heart. To my great surprise, I was told, on my return from the vestry, that the

Church were unanimous in their decision that I should be baptized and become a member with them. My sister and I were baptized by Mr. Emery in May. When Mr. Emery spoke to me before I went down into the water, he said: "You are now going down into the water, but <u>You</u>, I am persuaded will have to go into the fire, (emphasizing the word 'you') but do remember this, 'When thou walkest through the fire, thou shalt not be burned; neither shall the flame kindle upon thee.' " I had never confided in him up to that time, but afterwards he wrote to me, in reply to a letter I sent to him after he had baptized me, and he even then emphasized the conviction he had that I should know much of the fire of temptation. He was evidently led of the Spirit to speak and write this, for it was truly prophetic of what I have passed through since then.

At the service, the chapel was filled to capacity, although I was unaware of it, and I was told afterwards that, when I stood by the baptistery, my face beamed with joy. I, of course, was unaware of that, but I had such inward joy and peace and love possessing me, to think that I should have been permitted to go through this ordinance, that I had so much longed to do, and that I was as happy as it was possible for anyone to be. I did not fear the water or standing up before all those people; that was nothing to me at all, even though I, naturally, had a great dread of both water and standing before people. It was one of the happiest experiences of my life. At the chapel at St. Albans it was the custom to let the candidate choose the hymn to be sung before the baptizing. My immediate choice was: "How sweet the name of Jesus sounds". (We used Denham's hymnbook and the hymn is not curtailed there, as it is in Gadsby's).

The reason for my choice was this. One day, years before, I was carrying some old newspapers, bought from an old lady (a devout Salvationist) who was one of our customers, in which we used to wrap candles, soap-packets, etc. when making up orders to be taken out for delivery. Some of these papers were the news-sheet of the Salvation Army, and I had never seen one before. On the top one I read one of the sweetest little obituaries possible, of a young Salvation Army girl, seventeen years of age, and what fastened itself upon me was that her last words spoken, as she was just dying, were these:

> "Weak is the effort of my heart,
> And cold my warmest thought;
> But when I see Thee as Thou art
> I'll praise Thee as I ought."

I had then a new experience to me. I felt my heart go out in a warm glow of love to that dear girl who was quite unknown to me. (I do not even remember the name I read.) Belonging to a body (creed), with whom I had never felt I could unite and yet, oh what sweet humility and love were expressed in her dying testimony. As I read it I felt such a strong desire that when I died, I should be favoured to leave such a testimony as that. I was then about nineteen years old. I believe I truly knew then what it was to love someone for the Truth's sake, to love one who loved the Lord Jesus Christ in sincerity. It was a truly lovely experience brought about in a few moments, unexpectedly and unlooked for, as I was just performing my ordinary shop duties. "Love is the golden chain that binds the happy souls above," and I had felt my heart go out towards one who is there, in warm love. Again, here a little and there a little, does the Lord teach His people knowledge of His Truth and Himself.

On Tuesday night (after we were baptized on the Sunday) we went up to bed as usual at about 10 pm but, in the very early hours of the morning I was awakened by hearing my father moving about in the next room, and then I heard him say: "I shall have to wake Elsie, I cannot keep on any longer alone." I rose up immediately, and went to enquire what was wrong. It was that my mother had been taken very seriously ill with a severe attack of a malady which attacked her from time to time during her lifetime. As I went into the room, the words "when thou passest through the waters I *will* be with thee" came back to me. I wondered if I was about to lose my mother, but she was spared to us through that and many other illnesses for many years. For thirty-six hours I applied the remedy ordered by the doctor, which was hot fomentations, these being the only things that relieved the agonizing pain that she suffered when attacked in that way. I felt, of course, very worn out afterwards, but was so grateful for her restoration though. As usual after these attacks, she was weak for a long time. She gradually, recovered strength. The business grew gradually and I was kept very busy in it. One day, as I stood by the counter in the shop, momentarily idle, this came as a sharp temptation to me, as I was thinking over my baptism. "What has it cost you to make a profession? What cross have you taken up? Now, if you were amongst ungodly people and suffered persecution for being baptized, that would be a real profession. But you know that everyone whom you love and who cares for you around here, are pleased that you have been baptized." It shook me terribly for a little while, and then I thought: "Well, I know my people are godly people, but

> "Parents, native place, and time,
> All appointed were by Him." "

And I began to answer matters in my mind. As I meditated upon the verse of the hymn, I began to have opened up to me something of the comfort that there is in the doctrine of divine sovereignty, and I was enabled to withstand Satan's fiery dart on this occasion.

As the business grew, an uncle of mine, who was very interested in the venture to add drapery to our business, was desirous that, if the property next to our shop became vacant, we should rent that also, (It was owned by the same man as our own shop). It was a fishmongers', but did not seem to be a paying concern. Uncle thought I could then enlarge the drapery side of the business and there doubtless was great scope for that in the district where we were, which was comparatively new and growing, too. Uncle was willing and desirous to advance capital enough that I could greatly enlarge my stock, and do the necessary alterations on the property. It only needed a door to be made in the wall between the two shops in the front, and in the dwelling houses at the back of the property, to make it quite convenient and give us the extra warehouse and living room that we needed. I was very desirous that the way might be made for this to be done.

We had many loyal and good friends amongst our customers, and there seemed to be a real prospect before us, if we were enabled to do it. I had a younger brother just on school-leaving age, and a sister who was in a situation at Hastings, but wanted to come home, as well as one who was working in the shop. I was anxious for it to be a large enough concern that, with the help of the young members of the family, we could make it easier for my parents in the evening-time of their lives. Already my father showed signs of fatigue and was glad to leave first one thing, and then another, of the management to me. I did most of the ordering and buying from the wholesalers. The one part of the business, which my father did by himself, except for some of the delivery, was the newsagency. Only when he was ill did I have to do anything of that work. My mother had one or two serious illnesses around this time. My father was also far from well, and they were advised by the doctor to go away for a complete change. My second brother, (who had lived in Coventry for a long time, and was in a good position in a large engineering firm) became ill, and had to go away from there to a different atmosphere from that of a manufacturing town. He took a business at St. Albans on the opposite side of the city to where we lived. It was nice to have someone close, though for them it was a severe trial. The business was not a large one, and their income was greatly reduced compared with what it had been when in Coventry. They moved to St. Albans about two or three years after we went there. I didn't feel to have quite the same sense of responsibility, when my parents were ill, as when I was there alone with them, because, if necessary, I could soon be in touch with my brother. After a time, my brother's health improved, so that he was able to do some other work and not be quite dependent upon the business, though, of course, he couldn't take a full-time post. After some time of stress, Mother became better in health and my father, too, was much recovered from his nerve trouble though, as I have said, he became easily fatigued, but kept very perseveringly on, to do all that he could. Our financial circumstances had improved, as the business had continued to go on growing. Our weekly turnover had more than trebled to what it was in the earlier years, and in which we found the pathway very hard to tread. Things, too, were prosperous in the Cause of Truth. The ministry was very different from what it was when we were first there, and we were settled and at home, with no thought of any imminent change, apart from what might be with the growth of the business and, consequently, larger premises. Certainly, we had no thought of moving. In fact, my father was hoping that when they were older, one, if not both, of the younger brothers would be able to take it over, and the thing become a large family concern. It was a pleasant picture, as he viewed it thus, but we were to prove once more, our lives are in God's hands. "The lot is cast into the lap; but the whole disposing thereof *is* of the LORD." Oh, how vastly different are His ways from our ways, and His thoughts from our thoughts! Earlier in the spring of 1914, I began to feel that something of an important nature was about to happen. What it was I could not tell. I worked on in the business routine as much as ever, but I found that I could not look forward as I had done formerly, nor contemplate the increasing of business undertakings with the eagerness I had until then felt. This went on week by week. I no longer planned what I would do if we could have the other shop premises, or the various changes in the house and shop. Instead, I felt, as I told my friend at Chapel, (a lady member a little older than I was, to whom I was much attached, and in whom I often confided) that it seemed as though a big curtain had come down in front of me, and I could no longer look forward or anticipate things. This seemed a very strange way to take, and I wondered much what it meant. During the late springtime, my mother was ill. Afterwards, my father had a severe attack of congestion of the lungs. After they were recovered, they went down into Berkshire for a fortnight's change in their native air. They came back much benefited but, as usual when they were away or ill, much more fell to my lot to do. This time I did not get over the strain as quickly as sometimes and our doctor said that I must have a change and rest. One or two friends at different times had invited me to visit them for a holiday, but when I made enquiries, it was not convenient just then, as they had other visitors already with them.

I little knew, as I made arrangements to go away, what great things would arise from that visit, nor what lay the other side of the curtain, which as I have said, seemed to have all at once come down before me. But what did come about in the order of God's providence was, I am sure, according to His divine purposes and gracious appointment.

Upon the thread of what was (as I viewed it) a mistake in the ordering of my holiday, hung consequences which entirely changed my prospects in life, and opened up before me an altogether un-thought-of change in my future life – but this we know:

'All events are at His command.'

"HIS PROVIDENCE UNFOLDS THE BOOK"

Chapter 5

In July 1914, I went into Berkshire and Oxfordshire for a much needed change and rest. When contemplating the change, I had looked into the 'Gospel Standard' Supply List to see who was preaching at Grove chapel (Nr. Wantage) and also Oxford chapel, both of which chapels I hoped to go to on my visits there. My eldest brother, (at whose house I should be staying) went to Grove chapel, and my eldest sister (Mrs Hope) was then living at Oxford, and I should be staying with her for one part of the time. I found, when I looked at the list, that there was no minister for Grove, for my first Sunday away, but that my uncle, Mr. William West, would be preaching at Oxford for that Sunday, and at Grove the next one. So I said to my father and mother that I would go first to Oxford and finish my holiday at Wantage, then I would be able to hear a minister on both Sundays. As I was very busy with shop accounts, my father said he would write to both places for me, to tell them of my plans; which he did. I didn't see the letters he wrote, but quite thought everything was in the order I had wished. On the Saturday when I was starting, I had packed my case and asked my father to write a luggage label (as I was travelling by train). To my surprise he wrote it with the Wantage address. I said to him that I was going to Oxford that day. "Oh," he said, "I wrote to Wantage, that you would be there this evening, and asked them to meet you." Of course, nothing could be altered, but I felt disappointed, as I had particularly wished to hear my uncle preach again. I had not heard him since I left Wantage over seven years before. However, my brother and his wife were very pleased I had come, and I had a nice stay. I went with them to Grove chapel for the morning and afternoon. I was glad to be there again. It was indeed a place I loved, for I had had helps in that little sanctuary more than once in my younger days. The day before I left home, my father heard from a friend that a young man, (Herbert Dawson)

Grove Chapel circa 1914

in whom he was very interested, had been led into the ministry and, at the invitation of the deacon and friends at the chapel, would be preaching at "Zion" Chapel, Wantage, on the evening of the first Sunday I was in Berkshire. My father expressed a wish that I should go to hear him – which I did.

On my parents' visit there earlier in the summer, this young man (who had been a scholar at "Zion" Chapel Sunday School where my father was superintendent) and my father, had met. He had confided in him and told him somewhat of the exercises he was under concerning the ministry, though I did not know that at the time. I went to the chapel and, when he was speaking in prayer, I found my heart go with him when he quoted one or two verses of a hymn that I had often used as a prayer myself. It began: "Jesus, immutably the same," and as he repeated some of the lines of the hymn, (especially "I can do nothing without Thee") I knew that we were one in heart in those desires and feelings. He preached from Ruth, chapter 2, verse 14, "At mealtime come thou hither," etc. I felt it was good to listen to, and I felt convinced that God had called him to that work. He went as a boy to the same day school as I had done, to the same Sunday School, (when it was started at our chapel) and he was the last one to be baptized in "Zion" Chapel. This took place about 1½ years after I had drawn back from being baptized in the same chapel. After the service, when we came out, I was speaking to the few friends who were there, most of whom I knew well when living there. I don't think I spoke to the minister but, as we went up the street away from the chapel, a peculiar feeling took hold of me that, somehow and somewhere and at some time, his pathway and mine would be very closely together, so much so that I felt I ought to be walking with him then. I could not shake it off, though of course, I went in a quite different direction back to my brother's house, and we had some singing, and then a quiet, happy time together until it was bedtime. I was still under the strange feeling that I had had for many weeks, that great changes lay ahead of me, but what they were, or how they would come, I did not know. I felt that I was like a child waiting for a gate or door to open, to show me what was ahead.

On the Monday evening, I went into Wantage (about 1½ miles from my brother's home) on a small errand for my sister-in-law. While there, I thought I would go on another mile to see the house where we used to live, and on the way, call on three or four of our old Wantage friends and neighbours. I called, I believe, at three houses, but no one was at home, and so I called at one house (at which I had had no intention of calling), as it was very near. (We did not visit this house when we lived at Wantage because, while the husband was a very godly man whom we highly esteemed, his wife was of a rather peculiar disposition, and she never invited people to her house.) I was not sure, when I went to the door, whether she would invite me in, but she did, and seemed very pleased to see me. She had known us from my earliest childhood so, while she never asked people indoors, she would often talk to us when we were near to her gate. When I got indoors I found, to my surprise, the young minister who had preached on the Sunday, talking to her husband. He was made a deacon of the chapel not long before my father left Wantage and now that the pastor also had left, he was the one who was doing his best to serve the Cause by obtaining ministers and conducting services, etc. The minister had called upon him to make enquiries regarding some past records to do with Church matters. The deacon was not able to give him the information he wanted, but I knew that my father could do so, and I mentioned this. The deacon had to go out just after I had called, as he had a business meeting to attend. Soon after he had gone, as I had quite a long walk back, I wished his wife goodbye, ready to go. The young minister also did and, when we were outside, he asked permission to walk part of the way with me towards his home, which was in the same direction for almost a mile. He wanted to ask me about some things to do with the chapel, if I could tell him, which I could. After this, we began to speak about the things of God, and we had a very profitable time in this way. We were practically strangers, but we were able to speak of things in our particular leadings in the things of God. When the time came for our ways to part, we felt that we were one heart and mind in those things. I had, after this, a very deep exercise of mind come upon me. Often, in the course of a day, did I have to go aside and pray that the Lord would do for me, and in me, what was His will, though I was full of fears as to what that will would be. On the following Thursday, Special Services were to be held at Grove chapel, near Wantage, when Mr. Curtis (of Southill) was to preach. I did not know Mr. Curtis and, to my knowledge, I had never heard him preach, but I eagerly looked forward to the services, hoping that I should find some help and light upon my exercise of mind.

I went down quite early to help my cousins (the daughters of the deacon) to cut bread and butter ready for the tea. As I was walking to the chapel, by my uncle's water-meadow, these lines came very forcibly to me: "When thro' fiery trials thy pathway shall lie,..." etc. I momentarily stood still, for I wondered what did lay ahead of me, and it made me feel quite weak. I went on again and went into the chapel vestry, and helped them to 'cut up', wondering all the time what the trial was. We had not quite finished before the service started, which meant I was going up the chapel aisle as they sang this verse. "When thro' fiery trials thy pathway shall lie,..." etc. This brought a solemn awe upon my mind and deepened the exercise I was under.

Mr. Curtis' text was: "Weeping may endure for a night, but joy *cometh* in the morning" for the afternoon service, which made me feel that a path of trial of some peculiar kind lay before me. In the evening his text was: "And Jonathan Saul's son arose, and went to David into the wood, and strengthened his hand in God." When speaking upon it, he mentioned, among other things, how God's people were enabled to do this sometimes, when a brother or sister in the Lord had been walking a pathway of trials and difficulties (which he said "the wood" represented). By going to them, seeking to encourage them to wait upon God, to plead His promises and 'to trust Him with the clouds between' were ways in which one could strengthen another's "hand in God."

I was going on to Oxford after those services and, as I had to leave the chapel a few moments before the Service ended, I sat near to the back of the chapel. Sitting immediately in front of me was the young minister whom I had heard on the previous Sunday. A peculiar feeling came upon me that what Mr. Curtis was speaking of would be the case in connection with him (this young minister) and myself. How or when or in what circumstances I could not conceive, but I was convinced it would be so. The thought almost staggered me. I had never had any conversation with him (excepting on the Monday evening of which I have written) and I had not seen him again, excepting just then, as I noticed him sitting in the chapel. I left the chapel as the people were singing the last hymn and journeyed to Oxford. From Wantage Road station, for quite a little while, I had a compartment in the train to myself. As I was thinking over the Services, it came to me again, "When thro' fiery trials…" etc. As I was alone, I said aloud: "Oh Lord, what is the fiery trial in front of me?" I knelt down and tried to pray that the Lord would make plain to me what was His will for me, and help me to walk in the way He would have me go. I had another Sunday away from my home, which I spent at Oxford with my sister. They had a minister, but I did not receive any help or instruction on that occasion. All the time I was thinking of the "fiery trial." I returned home to St. Albans in a day or two and went back into business again, and was kept very busy each day. The next Saturday, my brother, Edgar, went to Wantage and Oxford leaving his home and business for a week's rest. He returned hurriedly the following Saturday, for that day (or on the Friday) war with Germany was declared, and the First World War had begun.

Now those of us who were in business were in straits. On this occasion, preparation had not been made for such an emergency. Our stocks were to be guarded vigilantly. We had to take stock of all that we had in hand, and on no account to supply anyone beyond the amount they were in the habit of having. This was an easy command to give, but very hard to carry out. In many places, where women as well as men work in factories (or in their own homes for them) the wives do not store jam and other home-made commodities. Instead, the only store they know is the shop.

People panicked and crowded the shops to take home all they could. When it was refused, threats were made to break into the shop and take what they could. We were forced to hide much of our stock indoors whenever we could, and continued to serve our regular customers as fairly and as well as we possibly could, until the first sense of panic was settled down, and people began to adjust their lives to new conditions. In a very short while, 40,000 troops were brought to St. Albans city, and a big contingent of them were drafted to the part in which we lived. We had two soldiers billeted in our house, and practically every house around for some long way, had two or more billeted therein. To add to our labours, we were told by the Commanding Officer of the camp close to us, that we must stock many items that the men would need, and we were asked to keep our shop open to a later hour whenever required to by the military. It was a time of trial and test in many ways, and our lives were lived at a very high tension. But even in this, we desired it all to be done in a God-honouring way. We were never required or even asked to open our shop on a Sunday. That would have been quite contrary to our principles. As fast as one lot of soldiers were trained, they were drafted to the battlefront, and a fresh contingent came. Our shop was on the corner from which three roads went. So it fell that we had one parade ground outside the Walton Street window, and another one in Boundary Road. The big shop window was in Walton Street and the smaller one in Boundary Road, but our front door (private one) and our living room window were in Boundary Road. The Sergeant Major (an old regular army one) who trained the Boundary Road Company, swore most dreadfully. He hardly spoke one sentence without an oath or curse. We could not get away from it and we were wearied and disgusted often, by what we had to listen to. We felt very sorry indeed for the men. Many of them, it was quite obvious, came from homes of refinement, and were as unused as we ourselves were, to this form of language. We often wondered at the patience they manifested, seeing this army was a volunteer one before conscription was introduced at all. We did all that we possibly could to help the men in whatever way it was possible to, by stocking things which they often required. My mother, at that time, was favoured with a period of comparative freedom from pain. She patiently, every weekday, baked large quantities of buns (or rather rock cakes) and we made gallons of lemonade with which to serve the men when they came off parade, weary, hungry and thirsty. It was customary, in those days, to have the shop, and the pavement outside, crowded with the men waiting to be served with these home-made things. We did this to enable those who wanted to, to keep away from public houses etc, and be able to get refreshment quickly which would do them no harm. We were often thanked for it, and appreciation was shown by the uniformly good behaviour of all those who frequented the shop. From the outset, we made it plain that no swearing or ill behaviour would be tolerated, and in a very short while they sorted themselves out, so that those who did not want to conform to our rules in this way, went elsewhere. One day one or two came in and started to be offensive in their language and manner to me, when one of the N.C.O.'s told him to go off the premises, as such behaviour was not allowed in this shop. They went, and I was never worried by that again. As my father and mother were both deaf, I had to do most of the actual serving. After a time, two or three of the senior men asked if they could help me by serving the others. This they did most efficiently, and I greatly appreciated the gentlemanly manner in which they treated me. We felt a great sense of oppression however, when we noticed that, while always well-behaved to us, some of them showed many signs of depreciation in their general behaviour. For most, the time of training was monotonous. Many of them had undesirable billets, and consequently, in their spare time, sought some recreation, thus often exposing themselves to much temptation, in many ways. Oh, how we wished that they knew the Truth of God, and that in them "The fear of the Lord" should be "the beginning of wisdom." There were some, of course, who regularly attended a place of worship, but the majority of them did not. On Sundays, my father would go out and distribute good literature among them. We had stacks of magazines which had accumulated over the years. These included: "The Friendly Companion," "Little Gleaner," "The Sower," and "Gospel Echo." As we went to Chapel, he would hand them out to the men in our street, several of whom, in good weather, would spend the evening sitting around our shop premises. We had a nice frontage within the boundaries of the pavement on the public street. They could sit there with my father's permission. Sometimes he asked them if they would accompany him to the Services, but no one seemed to want to do so. These things caused a fresh exercise of mind as to what the responsibility, of one who had made a profession, was to those who were so obviously 'without.' Natural timidity seemed often to make me keep silence, and yet, in my heart, I felt I would like to warn them. It seemed so sad to think of them being trained to go out to the battlefield from which they might never return (and from which many of them never did) without any apparent concern as to what death meant, or what lay beyond it. During the time I was at home, after the war started, we saw at least two battalions leave at midnight to embark on the train that took them to the seaport from where they went to France. On those occasions, public houses were out of bounds for many hours, so that the men should be sober, and well aware of what they were expected to do. We were asked (or rather told) to keep our shop open, and to serve the men with anything they required before starting. The few whom we knew to be professed Christians (although not belonging to our denomination) came in and warmly shook hands with us, and asked us to think about them. Many who had regularly bought things from us, came in and thanked us for the kindness we had shown to them. It was very evident, however, that all of them were feeling the strain and the solemnity of their position. Oh, how we wished that they knew, too, the comfort that only true religion could impart in such an hour. When they moved away along the street, lined by the people with whom they had been billeted, and others who had tried to be friendly to them, there was no martial sound of music. We watched them march out of sight, but, on the night air, the tramp of hundreds of them, down the long road to the station, could be heard. There was a peculiarly poignant and sad element in the sound. It made me think of death very clearly, and when the sound of tramping feet died away, and all the people went into their homes, scarcely anyone uttered a word. Many of those young men never returned. In less than a fortnight after their departure, one of the two who were billeted in our home, was shot down, when carrying a message from one officer to another in the trenches. Many others were quickly gone. We had at once to prepare for the next lot who came. Quite different from those who were with us before. The first battalion were of a London regiment. They were chiefly professional men, or the sons of lawyers, doctors, etc. Of the two who billeted with us, one was a son of an editor of a London newspaper, the other the son of the headmaster of a London Grammar School. The next lot were a Staffordshire regiment. Most of them were employed in industry. There were, of course, many among them who were very honourable and superior in their manners. Others were very rough and coarse, and it was very difficult, at times, to keep the standard of language in the shop as we wanted it to be. After rebuking some, and refusing to serve them unless they refrained from it, things sorted themselves out, and the orderly ones amongst them rebuked and reprimanded any who needed it, and helped us, as much as they could, in serving them. In this we saw God's care over us, and His hand opened on our behalf, and we were grateful for it, not only for our own sakes, but for the restraint it put upon some of the younger ones, for, by this time, young men of eighteen or more were conscripted. Conscription of a limited form was introduced, so that many of this regiment were only boys. We felt very sorry for them, and if we could, how willingly would we have saved them from the temptations to which they were exposed. These stayed for some time, and then were moved to another part of the country to complete their training. The next lot were the Royal West Kents. One lot which came, I don't remember who they were as I had left home then, were sent from St. Albans into active service in the Dardanelles. Of that big contingent of men, only thirty or forty ever returned to their homes and loved ones. Those were sad and trying times. But it is well to think upon them sometimes, and remember the price that had to be paid for the freedom we now enjoy. We felt the strain of it, greatly, in the business, for difficulties increased as time went on. It was difficult to get supplies to the shop, and difficult to ration them out fairly and justly when they did come. When, at last, rationing was introduced, it took the onus of the lack of supplies off the shopkeeper's shoulders, and people could then see that we could not do what they had previously thought we would not do. Nevertheless, strength was given as one day demanded, we were helped and sustained and preserved day by day. Sometimes it seemed as though, under the stress of the difficulties, and our anxieties concerning our own lives, in those difficulties, and concerning the country too, that other things were put into the background. Often one felt like David, "take not Thy Holy Spirit from me," and that prayer was heard and answered.

Chapter 6

After this diversion from the more personal things in my life, I must come back to them. After I had been to Wantage in July, my father, it seems approached the deacons concerning the young minister I had heard at "Zion" Chapel, and asked if they would invite him to supply for them at "Bethel" Chapel, St Albans. They did so with the result that he was invited to preach there later in October. As my father knew him so well and was so interested in him, it was arranged that he should be entertained at our house when he came to fulfil his engagement. My parents also extended the invitation to a week's stay, so that he could go from St. Albans to the next place at which he was engaged. So, once again, I met the one who, in the providence of God and according to His eternal purposes for us, was to be, in time to come, my beloved pastor-husband and life companion, though of course, at that time, such things as these were hidden from our sight. He came and preached and was made acceptable to those who heard him as one whom God had sent to preach. His text in the morning was Isaiah 48. 10, and in the evening Malachi 3. 16. In reference to this and the exercise of mind I had been under, let me here say that, an exercise of mind, which is truly indited by the Spirit of God, can never really die out. It can only come to a lively issue. Whatever it may be about, if of God, 'it lives and labours under load; though damped, it never dies.' In this particular instance, the intensity of pressure which all our new responsibilities for the time being brought upon us, and the long work hours involved, seemed to crush everything else. But that which is of God is eternal in its nature, and that which, by His Spirit, we are enabled to commit into His care, He does keep and it is in safety with Him. When our friend came to us, we were, through the kindness of a neighbour, enabled to entertain him at our house for a week. Our house was small behind our shop, and, as one room had to be given up for billeting two soldiers (my brother's room), we had no spare room or bed at all. My brother slept on a camp bed made up in the living room each night. One of our customers lived opposite to us. She was the wife of a highly placed naval man. As he was on active service, she was exempted from billeting anyone. She offered us the use of a bedroom at her house for me and my sisters, when necessary. She was away when we needed it just then, but she gave us the key when she went and told us to use the room. As I had no sister at home just then, my mother slept with me, so that I should not have to be in the house alone. One night when we were there, I was awakened in the night because I thought someone spoke to me. Mother was apparently asleep, but the words spoken clearly to me were these; "Commit thy way unto the LORD; trust also in Him; and He shall bring *it* to pass." I roused Mother and said: "Did you speak to me at all?" She said: "No, my dear, I haven't spoken." I layed down again, but could not sleep, for the voice had been so clear, and I mused upon the word which had come to me. I realized as I thought it over, that the Lord was about to answer the prayer put up to Him those months before in the railway carriage, journeying to Oxford. When I had asked that He would show me the way that He would have me to go. That word abode within me, and I watched and waited for the unfolding of it. During that week the men billeted all around, the whole battalion, were taken, by a very long Route March, to a distant place for manoeuvres. They were thus away for about four nights and as many days. This gave us some respite in the shop, and a little much needed relaxation. This also gave me a little opportunity to spend time indoors, and so the minister and I had opportunities for conversation. We found a kindred spirit to each other in many ways. On the morning that he was leaving, I was impelled, by some pressure within my heart, to write that text which had come to me, "Commit thy way" etc., on a sheet of paper and place it inside the cover of his Bible (which was laying on the sofa) before he came down to breakfast, little knowing that that very word was to be a help and confirmation in the way in which he, at that time, was travelling, and of which I knew nothing. Soon after he left he wrote to me, sending me a book which I had asked him if he knew of. I wrote back to thank him for it and a correspondence commenced, and was carried on from then. Around Christmas time he made known to me his desire for a friendship, and I knew then what was the new way I had to take. It caused much prayer for God's blessing upon us and, as we were one in heart in respect to both natural and spiritual things, we felt it was 'of the Lord.' I felt very happy and truly favoured of God in being the one who was chosen to be a companion to one of His servants. Also I felt a great concern that I should be instructed and taught by God's Spirit, so that I could be what I did desire to be, when we were brought together. A true helpmeet for him. As I believe, in answer to those heartfelt desires, I had from time to time, here a little and there a little, some insights as to what it would mean to be a minister's wife. The more I thought about it, the more I realized my own insufficiency. But then I realized that this was written for such as me: "If any of you lack wisdom, let him ask of God." When I mentioned it to my parents, my mother said: "I don't want to lose you, but if I have to, I would rather give you to Herbert than to anyone else I know." My father wouldn't say anything at all and did not for a long time. However much I tried to get an opportunity to speak to him about it, he managed to avoid it, and I knew, by his manner and his countenance, that he was not yet pleased by how things had fallen out, not because of anything he had against my friend, far from it, but because he realized that if the thing came to pass, it would mean an adjustment in his own life, as regards the carrying on of his business. So I had to wait until he had been given submission in this matter. My friend wrote to him as my father, stating what his mind was, but my father didn't answer the letter. Of course, as I was twenty-four, it was not necessary to have his consent. When I next heard from my friend, he sent a short note to say that he was going from one place where he was preaching on to another one where he was due to preach on the Sunday, and at New Year Services. He sent me a chapel Bill about them and said that he would write to me from there and let me know his address for the next Sunday, but, for a week, I heard nothing from him. I did not know where to send to him to make enquiries, and, as he had said in the last letter that I had had, that he was feeling very poorly, I became very anxious fearing he was ill. About that time, I asked my father whether he had written to Herbert. He said he hadn't, and I could tell that he was very rebellious about it, but I said to him that I felt quite sure that it was 'of the Lord.' In fact, I said this: "Well, Dad, if I am deceived about this, I am deceived about everything." He made no reply, but, as the silence continued about my friend's whereabouts, I had to pray almost hourly that I might hear from or of him. As it came to the end of another week and still no news, Satan took advantage of the circumstances to tempt me concerning what I had said to my father, that, if I was deceived concerning my leanings over this matter, I was over everything. One day, when in a short interval in the shop work, I went upstairs to pray that I might hear from or of my friend, as I feared he was ill, or had met with an accident. I had no means of finding out. As I came back down into the shop, this came like a dart into my mind, "Ah, you will find you are deceived over everything, for you will never see him again." It brought great anguish of mind, because I felt that I could not endure it, if I had got to prove that everything I hoped I had received from God, by His Spirit's work within me, was nothing, and I was deceived. I had said that, and there was the sting of the temptation. I watched eagerly for the postman (who there came three or four times a day) but still no news. On the next day, before the last delivery, I again went upstairs and pleaded before God that He would give me this token, that I had not been deceived in all that I felt He had taught me, but granting that I might have, that evening, some news of my loved one. As I asked, it was insinuated by the tempter that that was an impossibility, because a letter could not be written and posted and delivered in an hour or two, but I pleaded this, "before they call, I will answer; and while they are yet speaking, I will hear." As I went downstairs into the shop, this verse of a hymn came with comfort to me:

> "Though the vile tempter's hellish rage
> Will, with his darts, thy soul engage,
> God through the fight shall thee sustain,
> Nor shalt thou seek His face in vain."

The postman came that evening and I received a postcard from a stranger, to tell me that my friend had been most gravely ill for several days. He was just a little better, and had regained consciousness and had asked them to send to me to tell me he had been, and was, ill, but that he would write as soon as he could. It stated that he had an internal haemorrhage for three or four days and had only been semi-conscious since first taken ill. I could never describe to anyone the mixed feelings I had, as I almost snatched the card from the postman as he brought it into the shop. At first it was a feeling of intense relief, in fact, I said to myself: "Oh, I am not deceived after all", (as Satan had suggested I should prove I was). Then, after, as it came home to me how very ill my friend was, I felt, oh, so sad, and my desire was to go a railway journey to the place where he was; Bethersden in Kent. I suggested that I should do so to my parents, but they pointed out that, as the people under whose roof he was staying, scarcely knew my friend, and as I was a complete stranger to them, I could not do that without an invitation. Meanwhile, as a fully trained nurse had been engaged to attend him, with the help of others around, I should perhaps put a heavier weight upon their resources than they already had. On the Sunday, Mr. Janes (of Eaton Bray) was the minister. It was our Sunday for entertaining the minister and also, Mr. Janes was a friend whom we highly esteemed and whom I had sometimes been able to speak with, about my exercises concerning other things in my life. As far as I knew, he knew nothing of my friendship with a servant of God, nor the heavy trial both he and I were under. I felt, if he knew nothing, and I was comforted and helped in hearing him preach, I should know that was of God. As I was having tea, all at once another dart was hurled at me: "Well, you will find, in spite of all you think you have had to help you, that you are deceived, for your friend is dead already." I scarcely knew how to remain until the end of the meal, and I walked down to Chapel in a most sad frame of mind. I listened eagerly to the reading, which was concerning the disciples being taken to the mount of transfiguration and, as Mr. Janes read it, he emphasized that they feared as they entered the cloud. In prayer he spoke of that, and then when he announced the text it was this: "ye have not passed *this* way heretofore," and, while preaching, he spoke about the cloud into which the disciples had to enter, and their fear upon entering, and spoke of how, often, people feared when they had a providential cloud come upon them, and then he spoke of the revelation of what the cloud hid from the disciples' eyes, and how, often, it was that the clouds we have come upon us, and into which we were called to enter, often proved to be those that should break with blessings on our head. He emphasized too how sometimes one was called to tread a pathway that was quite different to any we had previously trod, and I felt a little strengthened and helped for a little while. I waited eagerly, and yet fearfully, for further news of my friend (meantime I wrote each day to him to try to help him in his pathway of suffering and weakness). All day Monday and part of Tuesday I waited, and then in the evening came another communication from the lady who had written me before, (the companion of the widow in whose house my friend was laying ill) telling me that there was a slight improvement, and that the haemorrhage had now subsided, but that he was still very weak and ill. (In time, he recovered enough to write me a few lines and oh, what a pleasure, of a twofold nature, it was to see his handwriting again.) During the severe strain of not knowing whether he had passed away, as was suggested to my mind on the Sunday, or not, and until I had the next letter from Miss Burch (as stated) on the Tuesday, I had been tossed and tempted, and yet, from sheer necessity, I was kept very prayerful for him (if he was still living) and for myself, to be given grace to tread this pathway hitherto unknown. On the receipt of the letter, my relief of mind was great. As I went into the living-room after reading it, the Lord spoke this word to me with power: "Now no chastening for the present seemeth to be joyous, but grievous: nevertheless afterward it yieldeth the peaceable fruit of righteousness unto them which are exercised thereby." I was able to commit myself and my friend into His hands. I found great relief in being able to write to him and, as stated, afterward when at length he was strong enough to write to me.

It appeared that, after preaching at the New Year Services at Bethersden, instead of going on, as he had hoped to do, to another chapel for the next Sunday, he was taken most seriously ill on the night following the services, with gastritis, enteritis and colitis. (There was a gastric ulcer too.) For several days and nights his life seemed to hang in the balance, and once the doctor said to the nurse in charge that he felt it would be wise to send for his relatives, and any friend he wished to see. My friend, however, felt that he would eventually be raised up, and told them not to send to his parents just then. The deacon's widow, who had him in her house, said he must remain there at her expense. Her married son and daughter provided the delicacies which he needed as an invalid, or most of them, and others at the chapel tried to help. It was some weeks before he was strong enough to get about at all, and it wasn't until after Easter that he could go back to his home. During this interval, however, as the chapel was next to the house where he was staying, (he only had to cross a lawn to get to the vestry door) he was asked to preach at some of the week evening services and Sunday evenings. In the account which Mr. Dawson wrote to the 'Gospel Standard' Committee when his name was added to their list of ministers, he fully relates his exercises of mind and subsequent leadings concerning the Church and people of "Union" Chapel, Bethersden, of which he eventually became the pastor. As the account is so clearly written elsewhere, it is not necessary for me to repeat that here. Only to say this; his very serious illness in a strange place among strangers, the kindness shown to him and the sympathetic interest shown by some in the Cause, were links in the chain of divine providence, which led to him being placed over them as their pastor and under-shepherd. That was in 1915. I am writing this in July 1963 just (by the date) forty-seven years after he was laying ill in the house next door to where we live now.

At Easter time, an invitation was sent to me by the widow, Mrs Pearson, to visit my friend, and arrangements were made for him to travel back home with me; resting at St Albans before leaving for his Wantage home. (I should say here, that when he was so very ill, my father was most kind and sympathetic and, as he was really very interested in my friend, and really attached to him, he was very anxious about him. He told me, as Mother had done before, that there was no one in the world who he would rather see me married to, but, as he dreaded me leaving the business and home, and what it would mean to him, he had never replied to my friend's letter, because he could not say, truthfully, that he was pleased.) I was glad he told me that, because I did want him to be pleased about it for I was very fond of my father, and I did not like to feel there was any cloud between us, though, even if there had been, I could not, and would not have taken any other way than I did. I felt it was the way God had prepared for me, and that I must walk therein. When I arrived at Bethersden, I was sorry to see how ill Mr. Dawson still looked, but I could see, by the fire in his eye and the intentness of his conversation, that (being raised from what, to all appearances, could have been his death-bed) almost his whole mind and purpose seemed to be engaged in the work of the ministry. He had not then received an invitation to the pastorate, but he was given an open invitation to the house in which he had been ill, whenever he would like to go there. We travelled to my home on the Wednesday after Easter, (I had gone down there on the Thursday previous to Good Friday). On Good Friday, services were usually held there, more particularly for the young people attending the Sunday School. He gave an address in the afternoon from the text: "And Joseph opened all the storehouses ....in ....Egypt." I had the privilege to be there and also to hear him in the evening, hearing him preach from Titus 2. 14. particularly do I remember the latter part of the text, "and purify unto Himself a peculiar people, zealous of good works." On the Sunday, he preached from Genesis 49. 19. in the morning and in the afternoon from John 6. 37. "him that cometh unto Me..." etc, and in the evening Psalm 92. 12. "The righteous shall flourish like the palm tree..." etc. On Easter Monday, we went together with some other friends, to hear Mr. Kemp at Biddenden, and Mr. Hickmott preach at Special Services there. While there, I met some strangers who, in later years, were to be in our Church at Bethersden, and who, even to this day, are our staunch friends, though neither they, nor we, realized what great things were to be done for us, or how, or when, or where, so strange and mysterious at times are the workings out of divine providence. After staying with us for a few days, my friend went on to his own home. He then, as he was given strength, went from place to place fulfilling engagements already made, and, from time to time, returning for a few days rest at Bethersden, for he had a peculiar exercise of mind concerning the people there. After a time, he was given an invitation to preach at Egerton, and he became more fully acquainted with some who were later on his friends, and so God's purposes concerning Bethersden, and some at Egerton, began to be worked out. Soon after, he received from the Church at Bethersden, an invitation to the pastorate. It was a matter of solemn exercise of mind to him. Things in the Church there at that time were not as he would want them to be, but several of them did not want them to be any different. As he himself has stated in his record, he did not at first want to go to Bethersden. One other little Cause he visited appealed to him very much more, and the people were very warm in their friendship. Moreover, the Lord had used his ministry there already, and blessed it to some. However, after many weeks of exercise of mind, he was constrained to reply to the invitation sent to him from Bethersden, and to state that, upon certain conditions (which were in accordance with his own views concerning Church order, and also strictly in accordance with the Trust Deeds of the Cause, which were sound and good) he would accept their invitation to be their pastor. As the Church had rather widely departed from the original rules, there were several things to be straightened, and he did not feel he could honourably begin his pastorate unless they were. This answer, with the conditions to be imposed, was put to the Church at a Special Meeting, and to the surprise of many, were conceded to, though afterwards, when the pastorate began, and the conditions had to be carried out, some rebelled and some went elsewhere, and some said that if they had known what it had meant, they would not have put their hands up. But the purposes of God were to be fulfilled, and Mr. Dawson had desired, for a token and confirmation that this thing was of the Lord, that, at the Church Meeting, the vote for him should be unanimous, and it was. The next few weeks were very full and anxious ones for him, for there was very much to be done that called for prayerful exercise of mind and very careful handling, and even then he had by no means regained even the small measure of health he did have before his last illness. He had some months before that illness been very ill with lead poisoning, and was told, as a consequence he must by no means return to the printing trade. As a result, the severe illness he had at Bethersden, coming, as it did, upon one already weakened in health, had brought him very low indeed. Mrs Pearson had kindly told him that, until he had his own home, he was welcome to stay at her house, and he received much kindness from her and her family (who lived in a neighbouring village but came to Bethersden chapel). After a time, however, he began to feel that he could not do all that he wished to attend to in his pastorate until he had the freedom of his own house. Consequently, he wrote to me about the middle of July asking me what I thought was the earliest date upon which we could be married, as he felt the need of his own home and a quiet room in which he could be quite private. My heart was in fullest sympathy with him, and I was anxious not to wait too long before our marriage, for he still needed careful nursing and very, very strict dieting. Now, however, I had to enter upon another part of my fiery pathway. When I told my parents about this, they thought we were hurrying things rather. We had had to do nearly all our courting by writing to each other. I had only seen him once in two or three months, but our correspondence with each other was very constant and, perhaps, in this way we could express our thoughts, especially concerning spiritual things, more freely than by talking to each other. I felt pulled first one way and then the other, while all the time realizing that, in this matter, one was my Master, even Christ. I must follow as He led me. I felt very sorry for my parents, though Mother was quick to realize that my first duty was in connection with the needs of my friend in the position which he was now to occupy. She sympathized with me, and yet felt sorry for my father too. He rebelled very much at first, though he knew in his heart that I was not doing anything wrong in desiring to be a help to my friend. The constant conflict of mind, as well as having still to work very hard and long hours, began to tell upon my health, too. At that time, however, the soldiers were put under canvas and, for the summer months, we were relieved of the billeting in our district. There were some of the more administrative part of the regiment left in the Orderly Rooms, etc., in the district, ready for any emergency return of the men to billets, but work and strain concerning the soldiers was greatly lessened, as they were camped about two miles away from our district. I was glad of that, as my father had become so depressed about me leaving, that I feared he would have another nervous breakdown. Mr. Dawson had accepted the pastorate, with this particularly laid upon his mind, that he would not accept a stipend from the Church, as such, but would have some boxes at the door, specially marked for the pastor, and whatever was placed in them would be his. He felt a special constraint upon his mind to do this. First, because he felt that was the most scriptural method, and also for the reason he realized, very soon, that not all who then attended the chapel were his friends. Some of the members of the Church were by no means well-taught, even in the elementary things concerning the Truth, and they greatly disliked the searching nature of his ministry. Others who were not members, but who attended the chapel, soon tired and went elsewhere. One deacon was quite antagonistic in his attitude. So Mr. Dawson felt he would be able to deal with them much better as a 'free' man, than he could if he accepted payment from them.

One day, my mother said, very kindly, to me: "Don't think I am trying to turn you from what you feel is right for your future, but I do wonder how you are going to live at Bethersden. Will they be able to pay Herbert enough for you both to live upon it?" (I did not know then what had been arranged concerning payment.) I did not feel in the least worried or anxious over that. That part of it had caused me no anxiety, for I felt, myself, that if the way for me to take was right, all that would be contained therein. So as Mother said that, the answer came immediately to mind: "Is all the silver and gold in St Albans, Mother, and are all the cattle upon a thousand hills, here?" She said: "Well, my dear, if you feel like that, I won't say anything more, but you will need something to live upon." One day, when I spoke about the future, my father said: "Well, you seem to have plenty of faith," (I didn't think I had) "but you had better be sure it is faith, and not presumption." He spoke rather bitterly, and I felt so hurt and cast down, as I was longing to have encouragement from some who had proved God's goodness to them. I was having breakfast, and I partially rose from the table to go up to my room, because I just felt utterly broken down and I scarce could keep from crying, when this came to me so sweetly, and with comfort too:

> "Rest in the promise God hath spoke,
> In all things ordered well for thee;
> Whose sacred words He'll ne'er revoke;
> Nor alter His divine decree."

I sat down again and finished the meal. It seemed such a solid restingplace for one who was weary and tempest tossed. I became rather poorly and worn with the attitude of my father. He said he could not nor should not, try to manage the business if I went away, though I reminded him that he had three other unmarried daughters, but he wouldn't contemplate that way of doing it. Meanwhile, the house that we still live in (at Bethersden) was built for the pastor to rent (the rent to be taken by the deacon's widow and to be used for the ministerial expenses). She told my friend that when we were married we should live there rent free, only we must pay the rates. He wrote to tell me this, as she was anxious that we should be married soon, as being of a very nervous temperament, she felt the responsibility of having someone as delicate as he was in her home. The question was, as it was a large house, how we should furnish it. For three or four years when first at home, as the business had to be worked up, I had only had pocket money given to me. I didn't mind that. I was so pleased to be living at home again with my parents, instead of away, as I had been for three and a half years previously, that I didn't mind not having a salary. The money that would have been used for that, helped my father, as, after paying cash for the business as a working concern, he had very little capital left, and it was necessary to build that up to enlarge stock and so on, as the business grew. For two years he had paid me a little more, but it was still small. I therefore had only a few pounds saved, and my friend had used practically all he had, to pay his expenses in Croydon when first ill. He was there some time, before going to his own home. Then, in trying not to be a burden to his parents, he had used up nearly all that he had. They were not National Insurance days, consequently there was no income, as he was not able to work, nor had he any from any insurance companies for sick pay, because, owing to the uncertainty of his health, and the fact that he had clearly developed bad varicose veins, they would not receive him into a Friendly Society. So we had very few earthly resources, but, at times, we were given a little faith to believe that the Lord would provide for us.

Chapter 7

I tried so hard to fight against the weakness that was coming upon me, but could not do so. I prayed that the Lord would straighten out my way for me. I knew my father could not possibly carry on without some help, and I did want to see the way straightened out for him too, as he was by no means strong. Then Satan again brought me into a low place, by suggesting to my mind that, if I really was a child of God, and if I really did want to do what is right, I should think of my father and mother, and not selfishly go my own way. He suggested (only, at first, I didn't realize it was his temptation) that I must sacrifice my own happiness, because we are told in the Scriptures that our bodies (lives) should be a "living sacrifice." Oh, how hard it is, at first, to recognize his devices, especially when he comes as an angel of light and quotes Scripture. It is well, when we have thus had his fiery darts to endure, to remember the hymnwriter's words:

"That impious IF he thus
At God incarnate threw,
No wonder if he cast at us,
And make us feel it too.

To cause despair's the scope
Of Satan and his powers;
Against hope to believe in hope,
My brethren, should be ours.

But here's our point of rest:
Though hard the battle seem,
Our Captain stood the fiery test,
And we shall stand through Him."

It was such a specious temptation, and looked so much like Truth on the outside of it, and yet, I had said, if I was deceived over my leadings concerning being married, I was deceived over everything. What was I to do? The conflict lasted for several days and nights and I could not sleep, and had become ill with the strain of that, combined with the strain of business and home life too, as my mother still had turns of illness. I had become so poorly in health, and the sleeplessness increased so much, that I went several nights and days without being able to sleep at all. The peculiar effect of it was that my body seemed to be drying up, and I wished, for the first time in my life, that I could cry, so that there would be moisture in my eyes, which seemed to be burning. My parents insisted upon my seeing a doctor. I did, and he, after close examination, sent me to another one. I went to his surgery two or three times, then one day he asked me to wait, as another doctor was coming to examine me too. They asked me several questions, and evidently thought something was worrying me intensely for me to be in such a weak state. I was given medicine to take. The effect of it was to make me drowsy very quickly after taking it, though I did not go to sleep, only became inert and unable to take any interest in anything around. After a time, the effect would wear off and then, by the time I had properly aroused from it and tried to have a meal, it would be time to take it again, with the same effects. I had to take it for four days and then go to the surgery again. Going back home that day, I felt so ill and strange, and yet so conscious of needing some help from God. He seemed so distant that, walking along the street under the heavy sense of depression I was feeling, I all at once said inwardly: "My God, my God, why hast Thou forsaken me?" As I said it, I realized that Jesus had spoken those words on the cross, and, just for a few moments, I did have a little meditation upon that wonderful mystery. But when I got home exhausted, and sat down on the sofa, the terrible feeling of loneliness and being forsaken returned. I had more medicine to take, this time much stronger than before, so that I became quite unfitted to do anything of a mental nature. I remember one day going into the shop to serve, as neither my father nor Mother, were available. A person required 1lb of sugar and a ¼lb of tea. I got it, but could not reckon the two items together. Mother had returned to the living-room, and I had to ask her to take the money and give the required change. She became very anxious indeed about me, and, after a few more days of taking the medicine, she put the rest away down the sink and said she would not let me have any more. It was, we learned afterwards, a powerful drug to make me unable to exert my mental faculties at all. It was done to give the brain a complete rest. In the intervals between the doses, when the effect began to wear off a little, I would be conscious enough to know that I couldn't worry. But I didn't like it. I said to my mother once "I don't like it, Mother. I do not know what is the matter with me, for I feel as though, if the most awful thing happened, I shouldn't really feel it, and I don't want to be just like a log. I want to feel things." Underneath, too, was a fear that I should lose hold of things spiritual, but here I had to learn, by these things, that the spiritual life of the child of God is in His keeping, and can never be lost. But I hadn't learned that then. Realizing that I needed more than any doctor could do for me, I left off taking the drugs and the effects of them wore off, and I became aware of my conflicts and perplexities again. One day, feeling that I must have some word from the Lord to direct me, I went out for a walk alone. My problem and my conflict was this. Was I to go forward into the way in which I believed God was leading me, and which my whole heart cried out to do, (for I dearly loved my friend,) or was I to sacrifice my own desires and stay back for the sake of my parents? Satan still suggested I was selfish to go on. As I walked by the side of the river at St. Albans, the conflict was so great that I was almost unconscious of where I was. My cry was: "shew me now Thy way," oh Lord. All at once, it was as though a voice spoke loudly to me: "to obey *is* better than sacrifice." I stopped dead and said aloud: "Oh, I am so glad, Lord, oh, thank you," and then I found that I was right on the verge of the bank, and if I had taken one more step, I would have gone into the river. There was no one else near at all. This double salvation, as it were, of mind and body, so awed me that I trembled very much but, with the heavy pressure of mind lifted and with the conflict for the time being ended, I began to feel better and walked back home (quite a long way, for I had walked on and on, when tossed in my mind, unaware of the distance). From then on I began to get better, though the weakness of the physical and nervous state did not pass away quickly. In fact, I was so easily tired out that I could not possibly do the work I had been used to doing for so long. My parents felt I must go away for a rest and change. I felt too poorly to go anywhere, myself, unless I could go to where my fiancé was living, but, as it was at Bethersden, I could not ask to go there. One morning at breakfast, my father suggested two or three places and I said: "Oh, no, Dad, I can't go there. Don't send me." He said: "Well, we don't know what to do with you, my dear, you must get away before you will be any better. Where do you want to go?" So I said, and it was a cry from my very heart: "Oh, I do wish Mrs. Pearson would send me an invitation to Bethersden, so I could be with Herbert and talk with him, but please don't let me go anywhere else." He said: "Well, I don't see how we can do anything about that, because we don't even know Mrs. Pearson ourselves. I said: "Well, don't worry. Let me stay at home a little longer and perhaps I will be able either to go there, or perhaps Herbert will be able to come home between his engagements." The very next morning I had my usual letter from my fiancé. He had finished writing it and then there was this postscript: "I was just about to seal this letter up, when Mrs. Pearson came into the room and said: 'If you are writing to Miss Aldworth, tell her to come here for a fortnight, that will do her good perhaps, to be in the country air for a time,' so just pack up your things and come as soon as you receive this." He had been writing to me at the very time that I had said to my parents what I would like to do, and which was the only change which I felt and knew would do me good. It was such a remarkable answer to my inward prayers and desires, that I felt and knew then God had not forsaken me. I had been quite unable to write to my friend as lengthily or as frequently as usual, but, though I had told him I was under the doctor for treatment for a nervous breakdown, I had not told him the great mental and spiritual conflict I had been under. I went down to Bethersden the next day, and returned home a fortnight later, much refreshed in body and mind, even though by no means quite strong yet. During my stay there, the sermon that my loved one preached on the Sunday morning was a great help to me. It was on August 15th 1915, Jonah 2. 9. "Salvation *is* of the LORD."

That gave me a real lift, and as a word in season is like "apples of gold in pictures of silver," so that was to me. One characteristic of the ministry which is of the Lord, is that the minister so sent, is ordained to speak, at times "a word in season to him that is weary." So many times in the seasons of conflict, which it has been my lot to have to enter into, I have been, oh, so weary physically, mentally, and spiritually, and have often felt one with the hymnwriter, when he said:

> "Tempest-tossed I long have been,
> And the flood increases fast;
> Open, Lord, and take me in,
> Till the storm be overpast."

A word from the Lord, a renewed sense of His presence (when for long He has seemed to be absent) is indeed as much a haven of rest as the Ark was to Noah's dove, as the same hymnwriter has written:

> "In the ark the weary dove
> Found a welcome resting-place;
> Thus my spirit longs to prove
> Rest in Christ, the Ark of grace."

When my friend and I were together, we could talk together of his exercises and desires for the Cause over which he was now pastor, many aspects of what that life would mean to us, came before our minds. The Church was a divided one, and the people were all strangers. We would not know, until we were amongst them and began to know them a little, with whom we could feel a oneness of spirit, and who those were who would have to be 'marked'as not really being one with us in the things of God and in the Truth, as we believed we had been taught it. I felt my utter insufficiency for the place I would have to occupy, that was, to be a real help to my husband (when we were married). Yet my great desire was to be that, as enabled. I knew that only as God gave me wisdom, would I be able to walk carefully and cautiously amongst the people with whom I should have to come into contact. On the Wednesday, (after the Sunday when I received help in hearing my friend preach) he and I went together to "Providence" Chapel,

Cranbrook. Mr. George Rose had accepted the pastorate there some two or three years before. There were Special Services there that day for the opening of the baptistery which had been built there, as the cause had been formed into a Strict Baptist, instead of an Huntingtonian one, as formerly. A Strict Baptist Church had been formed as quite a few had been brought to desire to walk in the ordinances as laid down in God's Word, and had been baptized by Mr. Rose at Mr. Kemp's Cause at Bounds Cross, Biddenden. Mr. Kemp had been one of the ministers who had heard the testimonies of the candidates, and had also assisted in the formation of the Church upon scriptural grounds. They were then desirous of having a baptistery of their own, but the peculiar design of the chapel made a difficulty, which was overcome in this way. The chapel stands well above the ground upon pillars, and there is quite a long flight of steps inside the door to get into the chapel, and a Sunday School is underneath the chapel. But after consultation with friends and with the builders, it was suggested that the baptistery should be built up between two of the pillars to the floor of the chapel, and made to be just in front of the pulpit, and by the deacon's table. This was very beautifully done, and when it was finished, it was decided to have Special Services at the official opening of the baptistery. That was left open for the day, so that friends (of whom there were many) who came from other Causes around, could see what had been done. I cannot remember either of the texts preached from, although I was very interested in it all, and was glad I was there. We sat up in the gallery. Mr. Picknell preached in the afternoon, but, while I heard and liked the sermon, nothing came home to me. Mr. Kemp preached in the evening. I only remember one sentence, but that was made good to me, and I went back feeling I had a word from the Lord. He said this: "You can't come too empty, and you can't come too poor." It was indeed a word in season for what I felt to need for my future life. Especially as, when he said it, these lines flowed into my mind, and I believe into my soul:

> "A fulness resides in Jesus our Head,
> And ever abides to answer our need;"

My friend, when he commenced his pastorate, did what he has continued to do ever since, to choose the first hymn for the day, or the evening service in the week. He did not know then what had come to me. But that hymn was given out at "Union" Chapel on the next Sunday, before I journeyed back home, and was a real confirmation of what I had received at Cranbrook.

On reaching home, I went into my room to write to my friend to tell him I had reached home safely and what was in my heart regarding the future, when this came, oh, so sweetly to me: "My grace is sufficient for thee: for My strength is made perfect in weakness."

Later on, when thinking upon the words which came to me by the riverside, "to obey is better than sacrifice," it was opened up to me in this way: "All true obedience to God's commands calls for sacrifice, but not all sacrifice entails obedience, nor is it that which, in God's Word, is required." I thought of the many nuns and others who shut themselves away, presumably to serve God, and thereby give up family ties and all that is dear to them, yet, in so doing, they have made a sacrifice which is in no way required of them. In doing this, they are in the position that it is impossible for them to serve God as He requires. The precept is: "By love serve one another," also, "we ought to lay down *our* lives for the brethren" meaning, to not spare ourselves in our service to them as God's people. "Do good unto all *men*, especially unto them who are of the household of faith," and yet again, "I beseech you therefore, brethren, by the mercies of God, that ye present your bodies a living sacrifice, holy, acceptable unto God, *which* is your reasonable service." Nowhere does it speak of a living death, which the lives, of those who are thus incarcerated, are. I have found the lesson then learned profitable myself, and it has been a help to others when I have had occasion to speak to them about it, in replying to questions put to me by those in difficulty as to the path they were to take. So again, "here a little, *and* there a little;" are we led into the Truth of God.

As it became apparent to my parents that, for a time, my health was not good enough to work as I had done, one of my sisters came for a time. Meanwhile, as things on the war front overseas became worse, older men were being called to the Services. I had a brother at Wantage, who was assistant manager in a large business in a village close by, which had been founded by the late Lord Wantage, to be a benefit to his many tenants and work people in the villages of Ardington and Lockinge and other places upon the Berkshire Downs. His age group was not yet reached and, as he had a family of six young children, we hoped he would not be taken into army life. Unbeknown to me, my father had written to my brother making an offer to him of our St. Albans business upon deferred payment terms, so that he could leave it himself, and take a light form of employment, and he hoped like that, with the regular payments from my brother, he and Mother would be able to partially retire in comfort, without being forced to take out what little they had been able to save against old age and enforced retirement. My brother was agreeable to doing this, and his wife was very pleased, as she, quite naturally, hoped that, as the business side would be his, he would be exempted from National Service. These things were being attended to and put into effect during the later part of September. Meanwhile, at Bethersden, my fiancé was meeting with difficulties, too. The house, which was built for a pastor to live in, had before been empty for over a year, and then a sister-in-law and her husband, of the widow to whom it belonged, desired to come there to live, as they were retiring from a farm in the neighbouring village of Smarden. She was a sister of the late deacon, Mr. Pearson, and their father had also been connected with Bethersden and preached there regularly, though he was not the pastor, and he and his family regularly attended the Cause, though living at Kenardington in a large farm there. When the application was made by this lady and her husband for the tenancy of the house, it was granted on one condition, and that was that if, at any time there should be another pastor sent to them as a Church, that tenant would at once move, and leave the house free, if so desired. When, however, this was asked for, he was unwilling to do it, although he had property of his own in

Bethersden village, which he could move to. This presented an obstacle which it needed God to remove for us. We had desired to be married in the late autumn, so that we could be in our own home in the winter. This problem over the house left us perplexed and cast down.

My fiancé had quite a few away engagements to fulfil before being able to begin his regular pastorate at Bethersden, and other ministers who had been engaged for Bethersden had to finish up their dates. Most of them came from a distance and had to be entertained over the weekend, which put a strain upon the elderly widow, and we were desirous of relieving her, by being in our own home. My friend wrote to me about the dilemma which had arisen, and I felt very sorry for him, as we could only feel that, while the man and his wife attended the chapel, he at least did not love or desire the ministry that my friend was helped to preach. This attitude of his was really against the pastor, personally. Then one day, I was busy and all at once this came as another sharp temptation. Satan had turned accuser now, by quoting this passage: "they could not enter in because of unbelief." He was not slow to bring back to my mind all my previous fears and faintings (although he himself had been the cause of them). For a time, I sank rather low and, one day in my room, I said to myself: "I wonder why it is that the time that should be most pleasurable, and is so to many girls, in my instance is proving to be such a time of conflict?" I did feel that I wanted the Lord to show me the why and wherefore of it all. I remember that, as Satan presented that to my mind, it forced tears to my eyes, for it was a very sharp shaft. All at once, this came to my mind and steadied it. "Well, it might be this. If you and your friend marry and, as the outcome of that marriage, some of God's elect are born into this world to be, later on, called by His grace, Satan will oppose right to the last." It threw some light upon it then, and I felt strengthened, though by no means strong in faith. I did feel though that I could say, and I did, "Oh, Lord, Thou knowest my heart in this matter, and that I do sincerely desire to walk in the way Thou has appointed for me, and no other."

This trial went on for some time, during which, one day, I went to a wedding of one who attended St. Albans chapel. A girl I knew well was marrying someone much older than herself, of another denomination. Everything had seemed to go so smoothly for her, though I knew that she was not concerned about being unequally yoked with one who, though a very upright man, would not want to, nor did he, worship in our little Cause there. As I sat in the chapel, I thought of all the set-backs we were meeting; my friend and I. The words in Malachi, spoken by the rebellious children of Israel against their God, came into my mind, too (and for a while I felt rebellious also), "now we call the proud happy; .... *they that* tempt God are even delivered." As I was watching, and saw how very much of the worldly conventionality had been conformed to in this wedding, all at once, this came with power to my mind: "be not conformed to this world: but be ye transformed by the renewing of your mind, that ye may prove what *is* that good, and acceptable, and perfect, will of God."

It seemed to come to me as an exhortation to show me how I must conduct my own wedding. What I must do and what I must not do, and it remained with me. My rebellion was gone and, instead, I felt how kind it was of the Lord to give me instruction. I felt that He was watching over me and directing my path. We had arranged, God willing, to be married on the 28th of October if our way was made clear, so that my friend could be at Bethersden chapel for the first Sunday after our wedding, but now it depended upon the tenants moving out of the house.

Very much had to be done at my home. My father had the prospect of a light situation, and preparations were being made for him to go to Croydon. My brother was coming up to St Albans for a week, to be initiated into our business and introduced to the wholesalers and their travellers and the customers, and I had to be with him there, to do it. I had so far recovered strength as to be working in the shop and serving again. Within about a fortnight of our wedding, the tenant of the Bethersden house expressed a willingness to move out, and did so the week before we were married. With this way being made clear, and so a pressure taken off my mind, I was able to concentrate upon all the necessary business to be attended to. My parents went on to Croydon. They were to share a large house where my sister and her husband lived, and lodge with her until the furniture could be removed. It had to remain at the shop house to provide accommodation for my brother, and myself, until his own furniture arrived the next week. My brother and I did the stocktaking, and went through all the books and ledgers, and finished that week. Father and Mother had gone to Croydon and, on the Monday morning, I heard from my fiancé about the obstacle being removed from our way, at the same time that my father wrote about the prospects for them at Croydon. My youngest brother had gone to Croydon with them. He was desirous of being taught the plumbing trade, but was, at that time, still at school, and would have to be for a little while. This made it necessary for a bedroom to be provided for him, and one for themselves. So my father wrote that, what was troubling him greatly was that there was no room for me. He felt so sorry about it, after all I had done for them. I was able to write back to my parents and tell them that the house at Bethersden was free and that, if all was well, we could now be married, so I would not be needing a room at Croydon. I thought how remarkable it was that I should be the one for whom there was no room. Surely the Lord had heard my prayer and made my way clear before my face. I had been able to go up to the warehouse a little while before and get the house linen, etc., that I needed to begin my housekeeping, and have it sent to a person in Bethersden, to store it until I went there. One last test I had to have before we were married. On the morning before my wedding day, my parents' furniture was removed to Croydon, and I had arranged with someone to come in and clean the house before my brother's furniture arrived. I had written to my fiancé to tell him where to come and what arrangements were made for his accommodation for the night before our wedding day and that I was going to meet him at the station, therefore, I wanted him to tell me the times of the trains. He answered the letter, but it was lost in the post, and I never did receive it. I felt anxious lest he was ill again, but meanwhile I packed my own luggage, putting little things that I prized, for safety, into my handbag, also the money (notes and cash) ready to take with me. At length, when I had finished, my fiancé arrived at the shop, so surprised that no one had met him. It was a great relief to know that he was well. I was to sleep in my brother's house (who already lived in St. Albans) and, as my parents were away now, I was being married from his house. My parents and sisters and all but one brother came for the occasion. Mother was grieved that she could not do all for me as she would have liked to do. Mr. Whitbread was ill, so we asked Mr. Janes to conduct the service at the chapel, which he very kindly did. He said afterwards that he had never felt so free at any service he had ever taken in that chapel, as he did when he conducted our Wedding Service. We came to Bethersden on the same day, as an invitation was sent to us to be here at Mrs. Pearson's house for a week or two after we were married. On the journey, I had an experience, again, of God's watchful care over us. (On the evening before we were married, looking round on my parents' now empty house, and picking up my handbag with my own little treasures in, I all at once had it come to my mind to give the treasury notes in my bag to my then fiancé, as a safety precaution.) When we got to Charing Cross, as it was wartime and the platform was very crowded, my husband said: "I will put the cases here, and you stand by them while I go to the Booking Office." I did so. I had two umbrellas to guard, too, and my handbag. To be sure that my handbag would be quite safe, I put it on my arm and held the umbrella with the hand on that side, thinking I could not possibly lose it like that. When my husband returned with the tickets and we moved to sit down, I said "Why, where is my handbag?" It had been on my arm just before. There was no doubt that, when I had been jostled by the crowd, it had been cut in the strap and taken; in fact, stolen. There were three different addresses inside, so that an honest person could quite easily have returned it. I lost my watch and watch-guard which my father and mother had given me, brooches and other trinkets, the cash I had, and the keys of my luggage, which had been sent in advance, but what cheered me was, that I had had it laid on my mind the evening before to pass over the greater sum of money for safe keeping. There again, I saw God's care for us. I was so happy in the fulfilment of His promise: "trust also in Him; and He shall bring *it* to pass," and He had done, that I could not and did not feel that I could make a trouble of the loss I had sustained, though I missed some of the lost property in the days that followed, but I was so happy in this, I had seen God's promise to me fulfilled, His Word was 'Yea and Amen.' All Satan's malicious designs and temptations concerning this had been overturned, and proved to be untrue and false. I felt to be most highly favoured.

When we arrived at our destination and I was shown into the bedroom we were to occupy (the same one in which my husband had been so very ill, and where he had laid for so long until well enough to get about again), the first thing that I saw as I entered this room was this verse, on a card hung over the washstand:

> "He knows, He loves, He cares,
> Nothing this truth can dim.
> He gives the very best to those
> Who leave the choice to Him."

I had never seen the words before, and I am sure my eyes were directed to them as I entered the room for, having read them then, they remained with me, and I didn't need to memorize them. I felt that God had done this for me, and had given me the very best. Oh, how good it would be if, at all times, we could believe this, because, He can do nothing less than this. He even gives that which is the very best for us to receive, in all His dealings with us, though we often seem to lack that faith which would enable us to:

> "Trust Him with the clouds between."

Having seen God's hand at work on my behalf and, in this particular instance, being brought into the pathway which, He had made it so plain to me, I was to take, for a time, I was favoured with a measure of peace of mind. I was enabled to leave things in His hand as regards ways and means as to our being sustained in our new home. I hope (as enabled) to write an account of our life during the 47½ years in which we have been favoured to dwell here, and some of the outstanding tokens and encouragements which we have had, proving to us again, that we were where He would have us be.

"To Him be the Glory. Forever. Amen."

Elsie Dawson

A PRAYER FOR SUBMISSION

Written after hearing a sermon preached by the Pastor at Union Chapel from Lamentations 3. 39.

Let me not murmur or repine,
    Oh Lord! beneath the cross I bear,
Hast Thou not borne The Cross for me,
    That I, a Crown of Life might wear?

'Twere just; if I should all my days
    Tremble beneath Thine awful rod,
And bear in Hell's eternal blaze
    The vengeance of an angry God.

But Thou hast cancelled by Thy Blood
    The debt which justice claimed from me;
Now Mercy shines on all my path,
    And Love does every step decree.

THY yoke then let me FREELY wear;
    ('Tis easy; and Thy burden light).
With sweet submission ever bear
    That, which for me, Thou deemest right.

But may I prove Thy Gracious Power
    To help - to succour - and defend; -
To keep me in temptation's hour,
    And guide me safely to life's end.

Bethersden, 1918   *Elsie J.Dawson*

THE LORD'S HAND NOT SHORTENED

Written in a time of trial after hearing a Sermon from Isaiah 59.1.

Can He, "whose every word of grace
  Is strong as that which built the skies"
(E'en though He seem to hide His face)
  Be faithless to His promises?

Can He who once to earth came down
  In love to suffer, bleed and die,
E'er be unmindful of His own,
  Or inattentive to their cry?

Will He, who shed His own heart's blood,
  To ransom us from death and hell,
Deny us any needful good
  While we as pilgrims here must dwell?

And can His power, so signally,
  And oft displayed on our behalf,
Be weaker than our needs today
  And less omnipotent to save?

No, no! His love, a constant flame;
  His Word of grace, forever sure;
Today, as yesterday, the same,
  Through endless ages shall endure.

And so this case beyond our skill –
  Too intricate for human thought –
We'll lay before Him, and we still
  Shall praise Him for deliverance wrought.

Elsie J. Dawson   *April 18th, 1920*

"Claremont"
The family home

THE MEMORY OF HIS GREAT GOODNESS

Chapter 8

In desiring to place on record the way in which we have been led since we began our married life on October 28th 1915, I would desire to extol the faithfulness of a covenant-keeping God, who has been our Help, our Refuge, and our great Redeemer, in all the trials of the pathway we have trodden.

"Not one thing hath failed of all the good things" He promised us."

My husband was led to accept the invitation to the pastorate here (Bethersden) in June 1915. From then he preached here when able, meanwhile fulfilling engagements away which had been arranged before accepting the pastorate here.

For the most part, he resided at Bethersden in the house of the aged widow of the late deacon of the Church. He continued to do this until after our marriage in October. We had to wait a few weeks before finally being able to come into our present home at "Claremont". (The name of the house).

We did, however, move in at the end of November. On first entering the house, this came very powerfully to me:

"I will all thy burdens bear;
I will all thy needs supply."

A little while later, my husband came in and, as he did so, the following lines came to him:

"My every need He richly will supply;
Nor will His mercy ever let me die;"

It was quite a long time afterwards, that we told each other this, and when we did, it was when we greatly needed to see God's power and love demonstrated in a time of sore need. Then it was a good word to us each! It would take a very long time to speak or write of the thousands of times we have had these promises fulfilled to us. (I am writing this 48¼ years after the promises were given.) I would, however, as helped, give some instances and also place on record some of the lessons learned; also the sweetness attending the lives of those who have to live a life of more *apparent* dependence upon God than the majority of people do. I emphasize *apparent*, because, "All creatures to His bounty owe their being and their breath;" and are dependent upon Him for all they have and are, but it is not so apparent as it is in the cases of those who have no immediate source of supply.

When my husband was led to accept the invitation to come here as pastor, he was given a strong promise concerning his pastorate, and that his ministry would be owned and blessed among them. Being thus led and equipped by the Holy Spirit's constraining power, he felt strengthened to take the course which was laid upon his mind to do, that was, to leave the question of being supported in temporal things in God's hands.

Two boxes were placed at the door marked, 'For the Pastor', and what was placed in them was to be his, this being quite apart from the general expenses of the Cause. The Church at that time, and the congregation, was comparatively small, and they were, also, a divided people. Some soon left, as my husband's ministry was too solemn and searching for them, they would have liked a smoother line of things. We had two deacons, but they were not in agreement with each other, and one was determined that my husband must go, as he, too, wanted a lighter line of things in the Cause.

There was much to try faith, and much to discourage, both spiritually and temporally, but the Lord gave to my husband and to me the measure of faith needed for our respective needs. There were times in the first years here when, in providence, we were brought into straits: during the first few months, we often knew what it was to be without money, after we had frugally tried to lay out the small sum then placed in the boxes for the everyday needs, and the weekly obligations concerning the house. One day in particular, I remember we had some bread and some vegetables in the house and, I think, a very small piece of meat. The meat and vegetables and some fruit from the garden served for our midday meal, but we had nothing to put on the bread for breakfast. We were, however, kept quiet, cheerful and hopeful in our minds and, after family worship, we started our breakfast with the pot of tea and the bread, when the widow lady from the next house came along to our back door with a basin of dripping which she said she thought we might like. She went away again quickly, and did not know, then, how opportune her gift was; it had come to her mind to bring it. We had a most enjoyable meal and proved it to be a good one, too. I could write of many such occasions when, in our greatest need, at the very time it was most pressing, the need was supplied. No one coming to our house ever knew, nor would have thought, that we were thus situated, and we agreed never to let it be known, only to the Lord. Then we should know, for our own encouragement, that it was indeed His appearing for us.

Once I was tempted to make known that I needed, as I thought, 2/6d, (12½p). The companion to the widow lady next door had told me we could always come to her (the companion) if we were in need and she would help us, but we did not do so, only that I nearly broke the rule that time. Going into the dining-room, I noticed quite a big pile of letters for post. My husband used to put them there if he had no money. If I had a little left, I would buy some stamps and post them. Things were very heavy going for my husband just then and I felt so sorry for him. I did not want to add to his burden by letting him know that I also had no money, because I knew he would grieve about that, for my sake, so I thought I would just borrow 2/6d for stamps from Miss. Burch next door, and post my husband's letters for him, to relieve his mind.

Consequently, I went to the back door of the house to do so, and she very willingly lent it. I came back with that and, also, a guilty conscience, a feeling that I had done wrong and that that was not the way the Lord would have me take. So I immediately went back and gave it back to Miss. Burch, and told her I had done wrong to ask her for it, as I had God's promise to plead, and it was dishonouring to Him to do that. (I would here state that Miss. Burch had done the secretarial and treasurer's work in connection with the Cause, since the death of her late employer who, when living, was the deacon of the Cause here and its chief supporter, financially. He died before we came here, so we never knew him.) When I went to the back door to return the 2/6d to Miss. Burch, my husband went to the front door and asked Miss. Burch for enough money, out of the general fund, to buy stamps for the pile of letters I had seen, which were really Special Service Bills for the chapel. I saw how very foolish I had been, as the expense was not ours, personally, at all. This happened in our very early married life, and it was a lesson to me for always.

During the first few weeks of my coming here to live, my husband had frequently to go, at the request of the members, to try to intervene in regard to another Cause a few miles away. He was still in very delicate health, and he had to do these journeys on a cycle in rather cold weather. I sometimes felt rebellious about it, as I feared he would be ill again, as there was the mental, as well as the physical, strain attendant upon it. However, he and another godly pastor went time and again to reconcile, if they could, those who had caused disturbance and disagreement in the Church.

All these efforts, however, failed, so those who had tried to have things straightened out and put right, had to reluctantly come away from the others. The result was that some came here and desired to sit under my husband's ministry, and some went to Biddenden to be under the pastoral care of Mr. Kemp who was the other pastor who had tried, with my husband, to straighten the things in their Church.

I have often thought how wonderful it was that the very thing which I feared would be too much for my husband's strength, just then should have worked as it did. These people remained with us from the very commencement of Mr. Dawson's pastorate, in January 1916. The members have all since passed away. (One by one they came forward and joined our Cause and remained honourable members until their death. The older ones who came out with them, but were not members, were later exercised about baptism and became members with us.) Now the children of those who came here then, are members, and some of their children are also, so it was according to the purposes of God that they should have come all those years ago. For a very long time after these people came and were joined to us as a people, there were some who criticized those who went to other neighbouring Causes, and it was even suggested that our Cause at Bethersden had been built up by the depletion of another one. This, of course, was very unjust, and certainly untrue, because no one was ever asked to come to our chapel and, more, my husband was bitterly disappointed that, in spite of all that Mr. Kemp and he had done to bring about a better state of things, their efforts had proved to be in vain. It was well that he could say, in connection with the criticism, "Oh Lord, Thou knowest," and to realize that He knew the end of a thing as well as the beginning.

As time went on, and he became known, many invitations came to him to preach in other parts of the country. He used to have engagements for week evening services in various Causes, particularly in Wiltshire, and some in Oxfordshire, when he was in that part of the country for a Sunday. (He had eight Sundays in a year away from "Union" Chapel.) This meant that he would be away from home for quite a number of days and nights before he could return. So it fell out that, when our first child was born eleven months after we were married, he was away then. I was many miles away from any of my relatives, so I felt very much alone. However, through the tender mercy of God towards us both, I was cared for most kindly and skilfully. I was not strong, but God had made all provision for me. I would not have felt it was right for my husband to cancel any preaching engagement, much as my natural feelings made me almost crave for him to be near to me when the baby came. But he was away in Wiltshire. I was extremely ill, owing to most grave and serious complications. Our doctor, however, was clever, particularly in such cases. Our nurse was trained, and quite proficient in her work and, during all that night, while I was so critically ill, neither she nor the doctor left me at all. Two or three of the chapel friends, hearing of the extremity, came in and waited upon Doctor and Nurse all night, fetching and carrying all that was required by them.

During that critical night the doctor said: "Put forth all the strength you have, Mrs. Dawson." I felt: "Oh, I haven't any," when this came so powerfully, "Thy God hath commanded thy strength." My baby came half an hour afterwards. I could not have received more attention had I been a queen in a palace, and afterwards, in spite of extreme weakness and exhaustion, I could not refrain from singing a hymn of praise to God for the goodness He had shown to me. My baby weighed 9½ lbs. She was a lovely child, and grew up to be a great help and comfort to us.

We had to travel a pathway of poverty, though this was not apparent to anyone coming into our house, which was a nicely built semi-detached house, about ten years old. There was a large lawn, flower-beds and a kitchen garden, all of which needed much attention, as did the many fruit trees. Also the shrubs and evergreens were not well established which, as every gardener knows, means careful supervision. We learnt all we could about the various kinds. I used to do quite a lot in the garden when my husband was away, as I didn't feel quite so lonely in the garden as I did in the house by myself.

I was weak for quite a time after my baby was born, and the doctor felt I ought not to be alone in the house, so we had a girl of 15, (Eva), whom the late Mrs. Kemp recommended, to live with us. It added, of course, to our expenses, and we would rather have continued without anyone else in our house, but it was doubtless in the purposes of God that she should come, for she was undoubtedly wrought upon under my husband's ministry in the last year or two that she was with us. (She stayed for six years). For a year or two, she caused me much anxiety because of her conduct in her time off duty. As I thought she was at her home about three miles away when her off duty times were due to her, it came as a great shock to me once, on opening my front door, to hear her voice in the street about one hundred yards away, and I knew that she was in company with those who would do her no good. When she came in, I talked to her of the danger and folly of that conduct, but, for some time, she was determined to go her own way. It was a great trial and anxiety to me, as I was young and I had young children to care for, whom I could not leave if, as sometimes, she came in late. At last I felt I could not continue under the strain, and I had made up my mind that I should give her notice to leave. The next day at chapel, a hymn was given out which had these lines in:

"Behold His patience lengthened out,
To those who from Him rove;
And calls effectual reach their hearts,
To teach them God is love!"

As the first two lines were sung, they so took hold of me that I felt I must show patience to her, for I felt very deeply conscious that the Lord had shown wonderful patience in His dealings with me, and so I left it. In time, she was shown, by an incident which frightened her, what an unwise course she was pursuing, and my trial over that particular care was removed. She later became engaged to a young man whom her parents knew, and left me to go home to a situation closer to him, until her marriage six months later. She lived, after her marriage about twenty-five miles from here, a useful, honourable life. I corresponded with her during the years, not very frequently, and she with me, right until her death. Her husband sent to tell me that, during her last days she frequently expressed her desire to be 'taken home.' When I read that, I was so glad that the Lord had shown me a 'better way" than dismissing her, and that He had led her into His Truth.

She came to me when Ruth, my first baby, was 6 weeks old, and remained until Janet, my fourth child, was about 6 or 8 months old. During that time we often had disturbed nights, as the First World War was on during the earlier time she was with us. Air raid warnings were very alarming. My husband was often away preaching. Once he had gone to Folkestone for the evening service, (after being at our chapel morning and afternoon on a Sunday); a raid took place that night. Eva and I and my baby were downstairs, (after dressing quickly), in the place where my husband felt we would be safest – in the dining-room. She was so white and shaken and frightened that I felt I must not show fear myself, (whatever I felt). I said to her: "Shall we pray that we might be kept safely, Eva?" She said: "Oh, I do wish you would,

Mrs. Dawson." So I tried to pray aloud and, while doing so, this came so sweetly to me, "Thy grace sufficed saints of old; It made them strong and made them bold And it suffices still." That abode with me during those dangerous days, and it often was a help to me.

Ruth was nearly two years old when my second baby was born. Before she (Bertha) came, I was greatly troubled, because I felt I needed a word of promise to be given to me, and I waited upon God for it, but I had to wait a long time. Then one day, it was given – just two words from the verse of a hymn, and I was able to rest upon it and to prove it true: "Seasonable aid." I felt if I had His seasonable aid, I should want nothing more.

The second baby was a smaller baby than Ruth, weighing 7½ lbs. My third child, David, was born fifteen months after Bertha. Just a fortnight before he was born, my husband had to be away, (he had been away for a week, before I had this experience). One night I woke up in pain, and with every symptom that labour had begun. I remember I felt: "Oh, what shall I do? Eva is too young to be of any help, and would be too nervous to go out for help." I was troubled most, though, because I felt: "Oh, I have come to this and I have nothing from the Lord to go upon." That seemed a greater anxiety than ever being alone in an extremity was. I asked the Lord to give me a promise that all would be well, and this came out with power: "I will strengthen thee: yea, I will help thee; yea, I will uphold thee with the right hand of My righteousness." I was so overcome by the magnitude of the promise that I laid still and contemplated it. We were 1½ miles away from the nurse who was coming to me, and 3½ miles from the doctor's house, and there was no means of communicating with either, as we had no telephone system in the village in those days. I tried to think what would be best for me to do, when I felt I could ask the Lord to so order it that it should not happen until it was possible to get help. He answered my desire and, upon the strength of His promise, I tried to rest quietly. Presently, pains subsided and, in the early hours of the morning I went to sleep. A day or two later, when my husband had returned, I waited for an opportunity to tell him of my experience and my promise. On each occasion I was interrupted and was unable to do it. This was on the Saturday evening. Early Sunday morning, when I was going to speak of it, I found I could not. Wonderingly, I got up and did the usual duties to get the meal, and get to Chapel without disturbing my husband in his Study before he went to preach. I went out into the vestry with my youngest child, Eva taking Ruth into Chapel with her. The service went on, the hymn with the verse in it, "I'll strengthen thee, help thee, and cause thee to stand," was sung, and then, to my astonishment and great delight, my husband gave out for his text the promise given to me in the week. Over dinner-time, how pleased I was to tell him what had occurred, and how I had been unable to tell him the day before. It was a great pleasure to him, because he had felt to be under a very special constraint to take it as his text. As he knew nothing of it, it was such a confirmation to him, and to me, that it was indeed of the Lord.

When my fourth child was born, I had a very marked experience. My husband was away preaching, but I was hoping for his return on the following day. On the day she came, I got up very early and sat in the dining-room. I was particularly anxious that one or two mountains in the way, in our household concerns, might be levelled before I had to leave it in other people's hands. I had it laid upon my mind to pray that my husband might be constrained (if he had got it by him) to send housekeeping money on to me, instead of waiting until he returned. I had had to order more coal, and that was due in that day, and I knew I hadn't the money by me, also the milk account was owing, (as often it was sent in irregularly). I somehow felt that both of these things would be done and settled before the person who was coming to take care of me and the house, arrived. I felt, as she was a person in the village, (not one of our own Chapel people) it should be done to be more to the glory of God. As every minister knows, sometimes travelling expenses nearly swallow up what he receives in serving the Churches. In our own instance, my husband has had to take what we had by us, to pay his expenses to the place where he had to be to preach, and then wait upon the Lord to be able, either, to

send or bring back something for me for housekeeping. While I
was sitting in the dining-room, waiting for the postman to arrive at
about 6.45 am, I had a spirit of prayer given to me, and a quiet
mind that I should see this brought about. "Before they call, I will
answer; and while they are yet speaking, I will hear." (Which was
a necessary promise if it was to be fulfilled that morning.) The
letter came, a registered one, containing what I needed. My
husband said he felt he must send it on, as I might need to use it
before he returned next day. Oh! how encouraged I felt. The coal
man came early, so I was able to pay him myself when he had
delivered the coal, (as he had to come three miles to deliver it, we
used to have 5 cwt at a time). Then I settled the milk bill, sent Eva
(my help) to pay for one or two more things, and saw things were
straightforward for my husband's return the next day. As I went
upstairs to my room, I did want to feel that the Lord was with me
and that He would, as before, grant me divine aid, and bless me in
what lay before me. As I went into the room, (one I did not
usually occupy) I looked at a text calendar which was on the wall,
and I read, "For this child I prayed; and the LORD hath given me
my petition which I asked of Him." My nurse arrived, and I felt to
be quiet and peaceful in my mind, and had a real hope that, like
Hannah, I should receive an answer to my petition – from the
Lord. As time went on, and certain complications arose which
increased my suffering, and as my little children were downstairs,
I was most desirous that I would not make any sound to frighten
them, by crying out in my pain. I buried my face in the pillow,
and asked for (using these very words) "just strength enough."
Immediately, these lines of a hymn dropped into my heart, "Bore
all incarnate God could bear, With strength enough, and none to
spare." I began to meditate like this: "I am only human. My
suffering is great, and seems to be all I can possibly bear, but oh,
what must His have been! He bore all incarnate God could bear.
There can be no possible comparison between the two." As I lay
there, contemplating His sufferings, I seemed to lose sight of my
own, and I have felt that, for a very little while, I was favoured to
have 'fellowship with Him in His sufferings.' These are favoured

times to look back upon, for then we can lose sight, for a little while, of all earthly cares and sufferings, and "consider Him." My baby came, and though for some days I was very poorly, yet once more we, my husband and I, had cause to bless God for His goodness and His faithfulness.

Chapter 9

During all these "times" – times of trial and of grief, but equally, times of triumph and relief, in our private life, with our family and providential cares. My husband had many proofs that his ministry was being blessed and owned of God, particularly at Bethersden, and also in other places. Several were added to our Church, and numbers gradually increased, notwithstanding that, some left because they did not like the searching nature of the ministry, some were removed in providence and some were removed by death. We had much to encourage us and to confirm us in our hope that the Lord Himself had "placed" us. His Word declares; "and I will place them." We greatly needed it, because, while to live a life of direct dependence upon God for everything we needed is a very privileged life, yet there must necessarily be much trial of faith. We never did know what our weekly income would be, nor how other things, such as clothing, household requirements, doctor's bills, rates and rent, would be provided – but they always were. One thing it did was to make us greatly prize what we had, and to use it carefully and prayerfully. To this day, it grieves me to see anything wasted or clothing discarded. I think of the days when I should have been so pleased with what are discarded so readily by some. There is a particular sweetness in receiving from the Lord that which one needed, and yet could not see how it would be provided. I have seen it in large things, and equally so in small ones. And I have felt as much, or perhaps even more, gratitude when the smallest items have been provided, as it seemed so very kind and condescending of the Lord. When one thought of His majesty as King of kings and Lord of lords, it seemed almost incomprehensible to think of Him, who alone knew of the need, that He should condescend to take notice of the smallest needs of sinners like you and me. If anything of a providential nature is calculated to soften and humble one's spirit before Him, it is that. One lesson we should learn from this – how necessary it is that we, who desire to be His followers, should be, in our measure, faithful even in the smallest things. About this time, I had an experience which I would like to place on record for others to be encouraged thereby.

For quite a long time, I had been tempted that all I knew of the things of God was to do with the temporal aspect, and not the spiritual, and I really feared that it was so. One day, I was making beds and was alone in the bedroom, I had been thinking about the work of the Lord Jesus Christ, when, all at once, this came so sweetly to me:

> "He, beneath the Spirit's sealing
> Stands thy great High Priest with God."

Oh, how I did prize those words, they seemed to give me a new hope in God, and I remember saying aloud (as I was alone) "Well, that is not to do with temporal things – that is spiritual." After a few sweet moments in which faith and hope and love all seemed revived and bright, the suggestion came to my mind: "You just remembered that hymn, that is why it came into your mind, you know you have a good memory for hymns." But I felt I could not let it go like that, and so I knelt down by the bedside and asked the Lord that, if it really had been given to me by the Spirit, He would constrain the deacon to give out the hymn, which contained the lines, at the next Sunday morning service. (We used Steven's Hymnbook then, according to our Trust Deeds, as our Church was founded, and worship carried on, before Gadsby's Hymnbook was published, and the hymn containing the lines was in the book which we then used.) I had this special time on the Tuesday morning, and I felt that the Lord had heard and would answer my prayer. As the week wore on, the many duties that I had to attend to took up much of my time and thoughts. My children were very small, the youngest being only about three or four months old. As usual, we got everything as ready as possible for the Sunday, as I had made it a rule that, whenever my husband had to preach, as far as it was possible there should not be anything to worry him in connection with home duties. I felt that a minister has much to burden him, as he contemplates the work of the ministry, that he should be freed from anything else. That Sunday morning, things worked fairly smoothly. (I used to rise earlier on Sunday morning, and get my baby bathed and dressed and fed in the bedroom, so that I could get the other little ones dressed and made ready for Sunday School and Chapel, with Eva's help, of course. Then, after breakfast, we would lay the tables, all quite ready for dinner-time. When it was Chapel time, Eva would go over with the older children, and I would start out last of all to go into the vestry with my baby, after I had given my baby the mid-morning feed). When the others were all gone that morning, and everything left ready for dinner-time, I went to get my baby, who was sleeping in the pram just outside the living-room window. When I picked the child up, I realized that, owing to a stomach upset, I would have to change it, wash it and do some of my work over again. I felt so disappointed, as I was by then quite tired, with all I had done in the morning already. However, I did all that was necessary, and gave the baby its feed. I am afraid I felt very irritated that, in spite of all my planning, I was so much behind. The suggestion came to my mind like this. "Don't go over this morning at all. You know you aren't at all in a right frame of mind to go and worship God. Just stay quietly at home and get rested for this afternoon." I yielded at first, but, as I sat down, I thought: "Well, if I stay at home, I shall only sit down. If I go over to the vestry, I can sit down and be resting there equally as well, besides, it is not right to stay away from God's house when one can get there, even if it is only for half a service." So I went over to the vestry. Strangely enough, I had not once thought on the Saturday, nor even on that very Sunday morning when I was getting ready, of what token I had asked of the Lord. When I got into the vestry, however, the last verse of the second hymn in the service was being given out, (the clerk, in those days, read the hymn verse by verse as it was sung) and this was what I heard:

103

"Seek, my soul, no other healing,
But in Jesus' balmy blood,
He, beneath the Spirit's sealing,
Stands thy great High Priest with God."

The very words which I had prayed might be announced that day. Oh, what shame I felt that I, in the stress of many things, had forgotten what I had asked for earlier in the week. But my poor petitions had been heard, and were now answered. Oh, I did feel so ashamed of myself, and so humbled that God should have been so kind to my infirmities, and so gracious to give me such a sweet answer of grace and peace. It seemed to me that I was given a double answer to prayer, inasmuch as, not only was I given the token I desired, but that the Lord fulfilled another promise He had given me years before, viz: "I know the thoughts that I think towards you, saith the LORD, thoughts of peace, and not of evil, to give you an expected end." This particular instance has been a waymark that I have looked back upon with profit and encouragement many times since, and instruction also. Here I would say to any mother with a young family: "By all means do everything in your power to be in God's house on time but, if, through emergencies, you are hindered, don't stay away." I would have lost one of my brightest waymarks had I not been delivered from the snare that Satan laid for me, to keep me away from God's house that Sunday morning. Never mind what other people think or what they say if you are late, so long as you have a clear conscience before God that it was not indolence or lack of methodical planning that caused it. God knows all about it, and He can and He does overrule all these things for our good and for His eternal glory. That should be our first concern – His glory and our eternal good. We were being led along step by step in our lives; my husband as the pastor of our Church and also a minister who travelled to many other places, which necessitated him being away from home very often. Our people, though loyal and doing their best, could not wholly support us, and my husband had been plainly shown that he was not to take up any secular employment to supplement our income. We had, from time to time, helps by the way, both spiritually and temporally, but there was quite constantly the trial of faith, and often we felt that we were, "of little faith". But God was faithful, as He ever is, and in spite of many fears at times, on our part, He did not leave us, nor forsake us, either in our Church life or in our home life. There was also constant anxiety concerning my husband's health, but in spite of much weakness at times, he was, for the most part, able to fulfil his engagements, both at home and away. He had encouragements, from time to time, in having those brought into Church fellowship by being baptized and joining the church under his ministry.

When Eva left us to be married, my youngest sister came to live with us here and to help me. At that time we had four children; three girls and one boy. My husband went from home increasingly, as he had invitations from many parts of the country. His ministry was blessed, and he had, from time to time, testimonies that the Lord had been pleased to use him, either for people to be called by grace under it, or to be brought into gospel liberty, or to be comforted and helped in pathways of tribulation; and yet, very often, the minister himself was cast down, tempted and tried, often feeling unfit for the great work. About this time, I was the subject of great concern over my own case, and also concerning our Cause of Truth. I felt such a strong desire to, "grow in grace." Also I did desire that we, as a Cause, might be settled and grounded in love, and established in the Truth. For many weeks, whenever I tried to pray, this language would invariably come to my mind: "That I may know Him, and the power of His resurrection, and the fellowship of His sufferings, being made conformable unto His death." It was real desire, real prayer, arising from a real sense of need of the very experiences contained therein. I have thought very often since of one hymnwriter, when he says:

"How simple are Thy children, Lord,
Unskilled in what they say;
Full oft they lift a hearty word,
Yet know not what they say."

And yet, is not true prayer, as well as true praise, indited by His good Spirit in our hearts?

"All our prayers and all our praises,
Rightly offered in His name,
He that dictates them is Jesus;
He that answers is the same."

In spite of the fiery trials through which I had to go in answer to my prayers, I do earnestly and fervently believe that He did indite that prayer, because he knew, too, how He would lead me into His Truth.

For some time before my fifth child, Mercy, was born, I was in exceedingly poor health. Some weeks after Janet, my fourth child, was born, I was taken ill with a very virulent type of flu, together with my husband and the three elder children. The Lord raised up a very true friend in the person of a member of the Cause, who lived in one of our chapel cottages with her widowed sister and her sister's child. She was, consequently, quite near to us. She earned a living with needlework and other domestic things which she was able to do. She, nobly, came and saw us through that sore time of trouble. Doctor said I must wean my baby at once, and it must be kept away from the infection, so I did not see her for 8 or 9 days. Our friend, Miss Susie Jarvis, undertook the right care of her, and feeding her with a bottle as well as the care of all of us laid up. A friend at that time had a whole case of oranges sent to us at just this opportune time. They were of excellent quality, and we were able to keep going, during that part of our illness, chiefly upon them, and also prepare them for the other three children, too. Also, as many people among us were laid up with the same epidemic, we could share the kindness of our friend and the goodness of our God to us, with our friends in the Cause. The friend who sent the oranges lived several miles away and I don't think she knew that we were all ill, but she ordered them through a branch shop where she lived, to be sent from a branch shop in Ashford, our nearest town. While we all recovered, it left a weakness with me, and this became very evident when I was expecting my fifth baby. This made me very weak and very poorly when she was born. After her birth, which was very prolonged at the time, my doctor and nurse told me that, if I wanted to be well again, and to be able to walk with any comfort, I would have to submit to a treatment which would involve being massaged for a certain time every day, and then being bound in such a way that I would have to remain on my back, and be unable to turn either to left or right. I said I would be willing to go through it, as I did want to be able to attend to my duties as a wife and mother. Their treatment to put the misplaced organs of the body into their right positions was successful but, after I got up, I began to go down rapidly in health. I did not know what was wrong, but I knew I was very ill. Also, I was still kept in a very deep exercise of mind concerning our chapel, particularly, and my own case, and the strong desires I had about my husband as a servant of God. One Sunday morning when he was away in Lincolnshire, and my nurse was still with me, I awoke very early and at once began to think of my husband; where he was, and where he was to preach, and I began to try to pray for him, and yet I had a consciousness that we had something which lay ahead of us, of a solemn nature, to go through. I knew that a minister's work meant that he must "go through the gates" and "cast up the highway". In other words, it must be the outcome of having to taste, handle, and feel the things of which he spoke. At the bedside was a daily text book, containing a text and verse of a hymn for each day. I opened it to see what it was for that day (I was having to remain in bed at that time). To my astonishment, I read this: "The Lord hath need of him." I felt dismayed, for, just at that moment, I could only think of one interpretation, and that was that the Lord was going to take him from me and that, as I was bedridden, and he was nearly 300 miles away, that I should never see him again. I felt, oh, so desolate for the time being. I thought of my little children, my own weak condition, etc., and then I tried to pray. All at once, it came to my mind to read the text in the Bible, and also read the context. It was in connection with the Lord Jesus Christ sending to the owner of the foal, the colt of an ass, upon which He Himself would ride triumphantly into Jerusalem. As I was prayerfully reading this, (and the words, "The Lord hath need of him", as applying to my husband) this came with equal power and clarity: "The written and the incarnate

Word in all things are the same." At first, I wondered what the connection was, and then the Lord was pleased to give me the interpretation. The Lord Jesus Christ, as the incarnate Word, rode upon that foal, condescending to use one of the humblest in the species of animals, and hath said of it, "The Lord hath need of him," and the owner willingly let it go. The Lord, in His great wisdom, has ordained that, from the race of mankind, right through the ages, there have been those who have proclaimed and preached the written Word, and, in that sense, they carry the written Word as that foal carried the incarnate Word. I no longer feared my husband would be taken from me, but, as I laid in my room that Sunday, while the others were all gone to Chapel, I became aware that there was some trial that lay ahead of us, which He required us to go through, because He had need of my husband to have some particular branch of His Truth to be opened up to him and by him, for the help of His people, and also to teach and to fit him more and more to still fill the position of a pastor, as well as to preach in other Causes, too. In other words, he had to go through another "gate". I did not know, of course, what lay ahead, but I knew whatever the pathway was, I must of necessity share it, and so suffer. I lay quiet and comforted. In a few days he came home. A week or so later my nurse left, and I was able to get about a little, and to look after my smallest baby. A friend (Miss Suzie Jarvis) helped my sister to keep house. My husband had to leave home again for a few days, and, one day, I was feeling, oh, so troubled, as I was sure something of an unusual nature lay ahead. I went into my husband's Study and, standing by the window looking into the garden, this came powerfully to me; "That, 'When thy foes, death, hell and sin, On every side shall hem thee in, A wall of fire I'll be.' " I was alone in the Study and I remember saying aloud: "Oh Lord, what is it I have to go through? For what can be worse than to have such a trio hemming me in?" I felt shattered, and I was still weak, so I went upstairs and laid down. I found, day by day, that my strength was decreasing, and I felt that a heavy cloud was upon me which I could not rise above. When my husband returned and was once more at home, he came into the room where I was, one day, and told me of a trial which threatened us, and which, if it did fall upon us, would be a shattering blow. I felt physically sick, and I remember feeling like a person bruised and battered, in the prospect of it. Yet, underneath it all, I remembered how, for months, I had prayed that I might know Him, the power of His resurrection, the fellowship of His sufferings, and be made conformable unto His death, and I wondered, even at the onset, if that was the beginning of the answer to that prayer. After that, I had three very solemn and yet outstanding experiences. On the first Sunday after my husband had told me of what might lay ahead, I remember going up into the Sunday School, and my husband was preaching. (I had got my baby in the pram alongside the chapel, and I crept up into the Sunday School to hear a little. The Sunday School adjoins the chapel and, being upstairs, was on the same level as the pulpit, consequently one could easily hear.) I remember that he used the illustration of the disciples on the sea, where it says: "And it was now dark, and Jesus was not come to them." It so aptly described what I felt. The next Sunday, still feeling weak and unwell, during the interval of the services I thought I would walk quietly round the garden paths. I was still labouring under the sense of oppression, concerning the future, when this came to me: "the disciples followed afar off." I felt, oh, so condemned that I did literally tremble. I walked on, and then this came: "What, could ye not watch with Me one hour?" This seemed to take every little bit of strength from me, and I was so weak, that I went indoors and upstairs, and my husband said that I must go to bed. I couldn't then tell him what I was going through, only that I remember saying, as I started to undress: "Oh, the disciples followed afar off. Oh what about me?" That same evening I had a very solemn experience. My husband had to go to Grafty Green to preach in the evening. The children were in bed and asleep, and my baby had settled down. My sister had the supper ready for my husband in the dining-room, which was just under our bedroom. I had not been well enough to get up again and, in fact, was feeling quite ill, but I didn't know what the illness was. I began to feel very cold, so cold that I couldn't describe it, and also a feeling of sinking and sinking. The cold gradually crept up my body, as though I were sinking into icy cold water. I had a stick close at hand to tap the floor if I needed someone, but I couldn't use it. I was quite conscious, but I could not open my eyes, nor speak, nor move. I felt that death was creeping up my body, and that I must soon pass away if the cold sensation went much further up. I heard my husband come in, and I thought he would be sure to come upstairs, as he almost invariably did if I was not well, before having his meal. This time he did not. I knew if he saw me, even if I could not speak, he would realize how ill I was. I heard him go into the dining-room, and I knew he was having his supper. Then I began to think of 'The power of His resurrection' for, all at once, this had come into my mind, 'Thou art the resurrection and the life.' I had a strong spirit of prayer come upon me that, as He was that, He could raise me up again if it were His will; He could do that, however near to death I was. I prayed that He would raise me up again for my children's and my husband's sakes, and raise me up from the deep grave I felt to be in. I could not speak a word, but oh, in my heart I could, and did, pray, and He answered the prayer. Shortly after, I began to realize that the icy cold feeling was not any further up my body, and, as that subsided, I felt as though I was being raised up. Presently, I could open my eyes and then move my hand. Later, when my sister brought me up a warm drink, I was able to take it and gradually came to. That was about 42 or 43 years ago, but I still remember, very vividly, every detail of that experience; of the power of the resurrection, physically. I was still very weak, and often had to give up. I was having, at that time, such intense pain at the back of my head and neck, that I often could not sleep. I remember one night, when my husband was again away preaching, I got every cushion and pillow I could find to spare, and piled them at the back of my head to try to counteract the feeling of my head being dragged back, the pain was so very intense. My husband had called the doctor to see me again, and the case baffled him.

One day, I was too poorly to get up, as I had not been able to sleep through pain. I was upstairs alone, and still trying to commit our way unto the Lord. I lay quite still on the bed. I had not even tried to read. I was still thinking on my previous experience during the past few weeks. The lines of the hymn, wherein He had promised to be a wall of fire, the feeling of shame (when He had said: "Could ye not watch with Me one hour?") which prostrated me, as I realized how I shrank from whatever might befall us in the cloud which hung over us, and over my oft repeated prayer that I might 'know Him', then when I had the experience, physically, of His resurrection power. I had yet to go deeper, and to prepare me for that, I had a most wonderful experience. As I lay like that, it seemed that all at once my room was filled with a most wonderful presence of swiftly moving living creatures. I did not see them, though there was wonderful light in the room, but I felt them, even a rustling as of wings, and then I heard the sound as of thousands of voices acclaiming the Lord Jesus Christ as He entered heaven. I heard this plainly, as they did it: "Thou hast ascended on high. Thou hast led captivity captive; Thou hast received gifts for men yea; *for* the rebellious also." I felt to come in here. It was, oh, such a wonderful sound, and I thought I was ascending with them, but, all at once, heaven seemed closed, the sounds of the praise and adoration ceased, and I found myself still outside. I cannot describe the anguish I felt, momentarily. I thought, "Oh, the resurrection is past. Heaven is closed, and I am left." But, all at once, the Lord spoke this to me: 'Thy life is hid with Christ in God beyond the reach of harm.' I had for a little while some apprehension of what the work of redemption was and meant, and what the safety of God's people was, and how nothing could harm that life which was hidden in Him. In what lay before me, I needed these experiences. God does not give us His gracious gifts and promises to esteem them lightly. It was His divine pleasure that, for many weeks after this, I had to experience what it was to be in Satan's sieve. Oh, it was warfare indeed! I often feared I should sink, mentally and physically, under it, and yet, I could not give up my hope. (I would mention here that, from my very earliest life, I believe the Lord taught me His Truth. Consequently I was never left, as some of His people have been, to imbibe the spirit of the world, or to seek my pleasures there, though I was kept conscious that I was a sinner, and I felt my desires go with the prayers in the little children's hymns which I learned and sang. Owing to this, as I got older, I often felt 'out of it' when listening to some ministers speaking about a law work, and relating some of their personal experiences, and tracing it out as being what must be known and felt. At one time, I remember sitting in the chapel and hearing the late Mr. Calcott preach in this manner and, as he went on, I said to myself: "Well, I haven't had anything like that," and I felt quite cut off. To my dismay, although I was a complete stranger to him, he came down to me, took my hand and said: "Now you know something of these things, I am sure." I wasn't able to say a word, but Mr. George Whitbread, who knew me and was close at hand and had heard Mr. Calcott speak to me, answered him to the effect that he was sure that I was taught by God. I got away as soon as I could, but it was often a trial to me that I could not speak of a definite call by grace. I was often tempted to feel that my religion was 'short weight', hence the prayer so often used, "that I may know Him" and how I was to learn, as Job did: "Behold, I am vile.") To return to my narrative, which I hardly like writing, as, like one of old said: "Remembering mine affliction...., the wormwood and the gall. My soul hath *them* still in remembrance." I became weaker in body, and dejection of mind seized me, and it was only too evident that I was in the throes of a severe nervous breakdown – so called. I was, indeed, walking in darkness and having no light. All the happiness and joy seemed gone from my life, and I felt to be forsaken and alone, even when in company. All past evidences of the Lord's goodness to me seemed hidden. Truly, the Lord had withdrawn Himself, as regards any cheerful hope and any comfort, at the same time. Satan seemed to mock my every attempt to pray or to read the Word of God, or use any means of grace. Yet I did still hope against hope. I remember seeing a lovely rainbow one day, and remembering it was set as a token of God's faithfulness, it gave me just a little hope and so, whenever I felt to be sinking in body and mind, I would pray earnestly that I might see a rainbow. I could not now remember how many times God answered that prayer, but I have thought many times since, how tenderly kind He was to me, battered and bruised as I felt with the buffeting of Satan. Our doctor became very anxious concerning me and, at last, suggested that I go away for a change. My whole heart cried out against it. I did want to be under the shelter of my own roof and near to my children, for, as soon as I was away from them, I became agitated, for fear some ill would come on them because of me. I was being shown, in a way I had never been shown before, the evils of my own heart, and the exceeding sinfulness of sin, and I was crushed under the weight of it, so much so, that, at one time, I felt as Job felt: "If I wash myself with snow water, and make my hands never so clean; Yet shalt Thou plunge me in the ditch, and mine own clothes shall abhor me." Oh, it was stripping work indeed. Sometimes I seemed to feel just a tiny little hope and light, and then I again I seemed to go down, even deeper, and every little vestige of hope seemed taken away again. It is not an easy thing to learn that "in me, that is, in my flesh, dwelleth no good thing," and to realize what it is to say, from the very depths of one's heart, because of a felt conviction of it: "Nothing in my hand I bring; Simply to Thy cross I cling." That is knowledge dearly bought, painfully (yes, very painfully) attained to. One can say from the heart then: "O thou hideous monster, Sin, What a curse hast thou brought in!" I remember reading in one of the late Mr. Philpot's sermons that those who have never known a deep law work in the beginnings of the work of grace in their hearts, were often allowed, later on in their lives, to be brought under great temptation from the great enemy of souls, as to the reality of their profession, and to be, like Job, riddled to and fro with doubts and fears. To be led into darkness and not into light, and made to know the utter depravity of their own hearts, to be painfully aware of an absent God, to say, with Job: "Behold, I go forward, but He *is* not *there;* and backward, but I cannot perceive Him:" and, oh, how painfully, as you feel and fear He will be silent, and is silent, to your prayer which you say with the psalmist: "Be not silent unto me: lest *if* Thou be silent to me I become like them that go down into the pit." I remember when I was younger, before I was married, and, I think, before I had any thought or prospect of being married, that, one day, in my St. Albans home, as I got up from my breakfast, I had this text come powerfully to my mind: "I will give thee the treasures of darkness, and hidden riches of secret places." (I did not realize, at this time of trial that I was being led into the place of 'treasures of darkness' or 'hidden riches of secret places,' or how much, for the past 40 years and more, I have learned what treasures and riches they were.) Interpretations belong unto God, and He has been His own interpreter and made plain to me, over the years, the truths He has led me into, in walking therein.

Chapter 10

I would here say that, the threatened trouble that we feared might come upon us was averted, and when I knew it, I wired my husband, where he was preaching, that, through God's goodness, all was well. I thought that I should soon be well again, now that the cause of immediate anxiety was removed, but such was not the case. I went down to my parents' home at Bodle Street, and was there for five or six weeks. But, in my soul, it was 'a time of war.' Oh, how I longed for a 'time of peace.' I had to be led even deeper, not so much, now, into the evils of my own heart, in the showing of them by the light of the Spirit's teaching, but, for the time being now, to learn more of the malice of Satan and his subtle temptations. Every drop of comfort I received, any little ray of hope, any desire heavenward, were all fiercely contested by him, until I hardly knew what to do or what to say or where to go. I walked for miles around the lanes there trying to find some place of retirement, for I felt, all the time, such a strong desire to have communion with God, and that I might find Him whom my soul loved, and, all the time, Satan would suggest that, if I was one of God's people, I would never be in the place of darkness and trial that I was. One Sunday morning, I went into the sitting-room of my parents' home and played the organ, singing the rest of a hymn that I had heard my father singing to himself while he was getting ready for Chapel, "Come, Holy Spirit, heavenly Dove," etc. This verse seemed so suitable, and I sang from my very heart: "Teach us for what to pray, and how; And since, kind God, 'tis only Thou The Throne of Grace canst move, Pray Thou for us, that we, through faith, May feel the effects of Jesus' death, Through faith, that works by love." Then following: "Thou, with the Father and the Son, Art that mysterious Three-in-One, God Blest for evermore! Whom though we cannot comprehend, Feeling Thou art the sinner's Friend, We love Thee and adore." Just for a few minutes I seemed to be lifted out of my misery, and could really feel to be praying in the Spirit. Yet I soon was 'shut up again,' but I could not let go my little comfort in the remembrance of it. At this time, I heard a minister, whom I think I had not heard preach before, take this subject: "The devil shall cast *some* of you into prison,.... and ye shall have tribulation ten days: be thou faithful unto death, and I will give thee a crown of life." It seemed very much to set forth where I was. I remember how he emphasized the set time, saying: "Ten days, friends, ten days, not nine nor eleven, ten," and he spoke of enduring the tribulation. I heard it, and believed what I heard, but Satan suggested that it could not possibly mean me, for I was not the character spoken to. I sank again. Then one Sunday, crossing the road from my father's house to the chapel, this came like a soft kind whisper, "He hath not beheld iniquity in Jacob, neither hath He seen perverseness in Israel." Oh, it seemed too good for me. I, who seemed so full of iniquity, so rebellious, so perverse, but it was so sweet to contemplate. Then my enemy said: "Yet that is true for God's people, but you cannot be one of them." Oh, it seemed like fighting every inch of the way, contesting every little crumb I had, and yet coming back to my own sad state. My husband wrote often to me and tried to cheer me, but 'ten days' had not yet ended, and Satan seemed to take even sharper weapons to use against me and to suggest this and that course to take to extricate

115

myself from the despondency and gloom I was in for the most part. But my soul recoiled against it, and I felt I wanted only to do the will of God. Only to walk in His ways, and even though He should slay me, yet I would (if I could) trust in Him. At this time, too, I read this verse, and took it out into the living-room to show my father and mother,

"All thy wastes I will repair;
Thou shalt be rebuilt anew;
And in thee it shall appear
What the God of love can do."

Gradually I began to feel not quite so despondent, and a little hope against hope sprang up sometimes that I should yet praise Him, though so often I had to endure the malice of Satan. Though I spoke very little to anyone of all I was going through, those around me, my parents and friends at the chapel, could tell by my countenance that I was in distress. Presently, however, they began to wonder, and I did hear it expressed once that there seemed to be something mysterious about it. They wondered what I had done, and I must have done something, so it was said, or I should never be in that state for so long. It hurt me dreadfully, as it was someone whom I esteemed and loved. I felt, at first, that it was more than my poor heart could bear, but the Lord supported me in that, and I felt, with Job: "I would seek unto God, and unto God would I commit my cause." I did long to get back to my own home. I wanted to be with my husband once more, to see my children again, and to once more be in our own Cause of Truth. The Lord saw my desire and my weakness. He kindly remembered that I was but dust, and remembered my frame, and very soon the way was made and I returned home, not cured altogether, but also not consumed. (Satan, in his temptations, had ever sought my life, but he was not allowed to prevail. I was so anxious that the Lord would bless our Cause, but, as I felt to be so sinful, so far removed from what I wanted to be, Satan suggested that I should be the hindrance to any prosperity and suggested the way out of life. Oh, I felt so cast down, as I did want to go home to my husband and children and the chapel.) I opened my Bible, and asked the Lord to direct me to some word of direction and hope, and this is what I read: "Except these abide in the ship, ye cannot be saved." (In the Acts of the Apostles, the account of the shipwreck.) Oh, what a comfort it was, because I could go back I hadn't to do what Satan had suggested I must do. I was like a prisoner acquitted, and I said, in all sincerity: "Oh, thank you, Lord, Oh, thank you," and went and laid down and went to sleep peacefully. These are solemn experiences, not to be spoken of at all times. I told no one at all about this for many years, and then, one day, I told an aged minister, whom I did not know very well; only that he was a very godly man. He was so glad I had told him, he said, and I felt that, for some particular reason, I had to speak of it after some remarks he made to me. He was preaching at a Cause of Truth for Special Services, and my husband and I had gone to hear him. (I had never conversed with him before and I never heard him again, I think, nor spoke to him again). This was in the interval between the services, and he came to speak to me where I was sitting down, and began to speak of some severe trials he and his wife had had to go through together. He knew my husband, and knew that I was his wife. Afterwards, I told my husband, and gave him an account of that particular phase in my pathway of conflict and trial. I do not like to speak of it, nor even to write about it, and I have put off, for some months, writing any more in my little record, because I had got to this particular part of my life. Yet, as I believe I had it powerfully laid on my mind 3 or 4 years ago to write this book, I do hope that, if it should ever come to light, it will be to show that, while Satan may seek to overthrow a child of God, he is held on a chain and, to him is said: "Hitherto shalt thou come, but no further: and here shall thy proud waves be stayed?" (One thing I have left out was, that my husband sent a long extract from one of Mr. Philpot's sermons, which he had copied, to cheer me if he could, and then, at the end of the week, when the new issue of the 'Gospel Standard' came out, the same extract was alluded to in that. Many friends thought that it was especially applicable to my case, and were so glad that it was put in there.) A sermon by Mr. Popham on Isaiah 35. 1,2.

"The wilderness and the solitary place shall be glad for them; and the desert shall rejoice, and blossom as the rose. It shall blossom abundantly, and rejoice even with joy and singing:" etc., was very helpful to me, as were the notes of a sermon by Mr. Hatton upon 1 Samuel 2. 6. "The LORD killeth, and maketh alive: He bringeth down to the grave, and bringeth up." The pathway I had had to tread was traced out in each article. As is often the case, (in fact usually) my recovery from the nervous breakdown was slow. Sometimes, when overtired physically and mentally, I would feel as though I was slipping back into the darkness again, and I did dread lest it should be so, but I found that, when I took some food or drank some milk or Bovril, or anything to quickly nourish me, I began to revive again, and I realized that I had really been delivered from the hands of my great adversary, and that I should not again be persecuted by him, as I had been. Then one day he challenged me with this: "If that pathway which you have been on for so long was really a pathway of trial and temptation such as God's people are sometimes led into, then you would have had a very marked deliverance, so that it could be seen." I didn't realize it was another temptation. I thought that it was really true. I began, in my heart, to pray that the Lord would deliver me, if I had not been really delivered, out of the pathway of trial, when this verse came to me ever so nicely: "He restoreth my soul", with special emphasis upon the word "restoreth", and then this: "He knoweth our frame." I began to meditate upon these two words, and, as I did, light began to shine again. I thought that physically sometimes, restoration is slow, as it must of necessity be, nevertheless, it is restoration, and it is very real. So spiritually, His Spirit does restore life to what seemed dead before, but often, the process is here a little and there a little, line upon line. And why? Because He knoweth our frame. He remembereth we are dust. I remember people said to me, more than once, when I was away: "Ah, what you want is a 'dead lift'." I know, inwardly, I shrank, and I said to myself: "Oh, I do not think I could stand anything that is too great," but, oh, how I did crave for the sweet soft shining of His grace in my heart: the healing beam of the Sun of Righteousness. As one hymnwriter once wrote:

> "And though not like a mighty wind,
> Nor with a rushing noise,
> May we Thy calmer comforts find,
> And hear Thy still small voice."

I had one sweet little touch of that the very next Sunday morning. I had been helping to get the older children ready for Sunday School, which began at 9.30, while my sister laid the table ready for dinner, (for when we returned from Chapel at 12.00 noon). I had then put my baby into her pram and pushed it along the hall to the front door for her to lay out in the air until I was ready to take her into the vestry for the Morning Service. As I was there, I heard the Sunday School children singing. I could not hear the words they sang, but it was a well-known S.M. tune, and these verses came, oh, so sweetly into my heart:

> "Its bonds shall never break,
> Though earth's old columns bow;
> The strong, the tempted, and the weak,
> Are one in Jesus now."

The two lines, "The strong, the tempted, and the weak Are one in Jesus now," were like cold waters to a thirsty soul. Oh, how good it was to be able once more to feel I was one with God's people. I hope never to lose the memory of that 'shining of the Spirit' within my heart. All through that long, weary time of conflict, and over the weeks they lasted, oh, how I longed for the healing of tears. I wished, oh, so ardently sometimes, that I could cry, but I could not, but when those words came so sweetly to me on that morning, the tears came so readily. Tears like that are precious and most desirable. As I came indoors, the last verse of the hymn came with equal power:

> "Here let the weary rest,
> Who love the Saviour's name;
> Though with no sweet enjoyments blessed,
> This covenant stands the same."

Afterwards, when I could look up the hymn, 921 in Gadsby's Hymnbook, I found that every line in it seemed most suitable to my case. On the first Sunday after my arrival home, my husband preached in the afternoon from Revelation 3.12. "Him that overcometh will I make a pillar in the temple of My God, and he shall go no more out." For some time I had set-backs in which I greatly feared I might have yet more of Satan's malice to endure.

One evening, (when Mr. Dawson was away again preaching) I went up to bed early, in fact we all did, and remember earnestly praying, while I prepared for bed, that the Lord would keep Satan at a distance from me, and that I might be spared, if it was His will, from having to walk such a painful path again. And, after laying for some time, I grew quiet in my mind, and went to sleep. In my sleep, I dreamt I was going from one chapel to another, but all were full – there was no room for me, but at each one, they were singing when I got there, (and I heard it through the doors and windows) "For Jesus' blood, through earth and skies, Mercy, eternal mercy, cries." In my dream, I went to many, though I could not say what chapels they were, but it made such an impression on my mind that, in every one, the theme was the same. I felt cheered and strengthened, and at last I awoke and found myself saying aloud: "How sweet the name of Jesus sounds In a believer's ear! It soothes his sorrows, heals his wounds, And drives away his fear." That was an outstanding time. For weeks afterwards, I had almost constantly in my mind, either one hymn or the other: "Jesus blood," or, "How sweet the name of Jesus sounds." It seemed so wonderful to me, that the Lord should so have spoken peace to me while I slept. I did not have to go so low down again, but what I did realize was this. As I went on, and got further away from the conflict and desolation I had endured, I knew that the Lord had answered my prayer of years, that I might know His Truth, that I might know Him and the power of His resurrection. He had shown me what I felt I had lacked in my early teaching, and what some do learn in a deep conviction of sin under the law. He showed to me the exceeding sinfulness of sin, because of what it cost the Saviour to provide the remedy for it. I remember saying to my husband and sister, one morning soon after I came back home, that I would like to see written in letters of gold in the sky, for all to read:

> "Sin's filth and guilt, perceived and felt,
> Make known God's great salvation."

Only so can one truly say: "Jesus, Thy blood and righteousness are all my ornament and dress. Fearless with these pure garments on, I'll view the splendour of Thy Throne."

I have since thought that one should be most grateful for being kept in youth, and spared from committing sin outwardly, for, when the Spirit of God shines into the inmost recesses of the heart, and reveals what human nature is as the result of man's Fall in the beginning, one cannot really be grateful enough that He was pleased to preserve one from one's own sinful nature. It was, after all, the same gracious power which kept us, even before we became so much aware of our need of being kept. Oh, it is good to look back, now I am old, and view how faithful He has been to His promises given to me about 57 years ago, when I feared lest I might fall away, and get to the end of all my religion. "Who are kept by the power of God through faith unto salvation."

During the months that followed my deliverance from my path of trial and darkness, two scriptures seemed to fasten upon my mind with power, as I thought over the Lord's deliverance. One was: "As a beast goeth down into the valley, the Spirit of the LORD caused him to rest:" and then: "My people shall dwell in a peaceable habitation,.... and in quiet resting places." And many, many times since, I have compared the two experiences with a time of war and a time of peace. "When He giveth quietness, who then can make trouble?" Peace, His peace, is like a river going on, ever going on, undisturbed in its depths by anything that ripples the surface or occurs along its banks.

I would like to record here the faithfulness of God, as I remember how He prepared me, as it were, for the season of severe conflict and trial I had to come into. He did prove Himself to be a wall of fire round about me, as He said he would, when my "foes, death, hell and sin, On every side" did hem me in, and because He had "received gifts for men; yea, *for* the rebellious also," when I was permitted to have a glimpse of His resurrection, my life, my spiritual life, was safely in His keeping, beyond the reach of harm. All the malice of Satan could not touch it, for though it was hidden, it was safely hidden!

Since then, we have had to pass through varied trials and difficulties. When I returned from Bodle Street, I found my children well. My baby, which was with me there, grew and thrived, and became a bonny child. She now is a mother of eight children and is, herself, the wife of one of God's servants.

My second son, Peter, was born when Mercy was 17 months old. It was a great source of pleasure to us to have a second boy. I had a sense of quietness and hope that all would be well at his birth, but I had not yet received just that which I had desired of the Lord; not a special word! It was Christmas time and Mr. Dawson bought a small carol book so that he might be able to teach some of the carols to the older children. One carol was completely strange to us, but my children were standing around the organ singing the words as their daddy played the tune to them, and this is what they sang, and he did, too:

> "Christ who came to earth that morn
> In a manger lying.
> Hallowed birth by being born,
> Sweetened death by dying."

That was the word for me – that time. The Lord Jesus Christ had, "Hallowed birth by being born," so why should I shrink in any way from being a mother? It gave new light, still, upon what I had always regarded as a solemn, and yet sacred, experience. Peter was born a week later, and all was well! He was healthy and fairly strong, and we had much pleasure in watching him through childhood.

Things were still encouraging at Chapel. My husband was being helped, the ministry was owned by God, and there were some additions to the Church. His health for some years was a source of anxiety, especially when he had to make long journeys from home. The Lord was better to me than my many fears had suggested He would be. At the time my seventh child, Joyce, was born, (a year and nine months after Peter), my husband was greatly cheered to know that his younger sister, Mary, who was in business in Luton, had been called by grace, and had been led to join the Church at "Bethel", Luton, then under the pastoral care of Mr. Crawford Fookes. We named our baby, Joyce Mary, as, at that time, my husband felt he could: "Rejoice in the Lord." We had the nearest name we could get to that word. She was a particularly happy baby, with a very sunny temperament.

Between her birth and that of Lois, the next child, I had to experience the loss of my mother, a most gracious woman whom I most dearly loved. Before this, and indeed just about the time of Joyce's birth, my sister had left us to be married. (She married a young man who was a member of our Church – she was also a member.) In her place, my eldest brother's eldest daughter came to live with us. She came from Croydon, where her father then lived, and her coming to us then, was the means whereby she and her husband met – he was the second son of one of our deacons then, who has since passed away. John is now one of our deacons, and she is indeed a very able and desirable deacon's wife, always ready to do what she can to support her husband, in a practical way, in running the Cause. They were both baptized by my husband. I believe she became a member before their courtship began, because I remember that John, in giving his testimony, said that he did desire, prayerfully, that the Lord would raise up a friend for him who did love the Lord, and he believed and knew she did, and that he had been able to commence the friendship with her. She was a great help to me in the sorrowful days of my mother's illness and death, which followed grave injuries received by a fall downstairs. We were sent for, to go to Bodle Street, and I watched her during the whole of the night preceding her death. Her sufferings had been intense, and the Doctor had injected a drug to alleviate the pain for a time. He came in the evening to inject again, and I said to him, as he did it: "Will my mother rouse again from the effects of this drug?" He replied: "You wouldn't like her to wake to intense pain and suffering, would you? That is what it will be if she does." I said: "Well, I don't wish that. I would rather that she was taken from her suffering."

Nevertheless, I watched all night, hoping she would just speak to us again, but the heavy breathing continued all night. But, at about twenty to seven in the morning, she roused, opened her eyes and looked around on all of us who were there. My eldest brother, who lived the furthest away, had not then arrived. She evidently missed him, but as she looked around, a most lovely smile came over her face and then, looking again on us all, and smiling on each, she looked up into the room above her, and she was seeing, we knew, something far above what we could see. Her face was radiant with a heavenly beauty, which was almost indescribably lovely. I had never seen, nor have I since, such a countenance of joy and full felicity. It did not need words, but, if she could have spoken, I think she would have expressed, among other things, the great wonder that she felt, as she undoubtedly gazed into heaven, that she had safely arrived there.

She had had a life of much suffering for nearly all of her life since I could remember. They (my parents) had trod poverty's vale, and had had much anxiety and care, as she strove to do all she could to bring her large family up in the fear of the Lord. Quiet and unassuming, she never spoke very much about her feelings, but she was one who truly feared God above many.

I was not aware until just after this, that my eighth baby would be due about 7½ months later, but I knew that the two nights of fighting sleep to be with my mother had taken great toll of my strength. I returned to my home and children, a friend kindly bringing me and my sister-in-law back to Bethersden. Before we came away, however, and before Mr. Gibb came from Tenterden to arrange for the funeral, (we were having Mother's burial at Tenterden Chapel yard), my father, to my great surprise, said, as he looked around our living-room: "I shall not part with this and that." I said to him: "Don't think even of parting with anything, Dad. We would like you to have things as you have always had them. There is no need for anything to be moved or altered." He replied: "I shall not stay here now that your mother is gone. There is nothing to keep me here, that is why I said I wouldn't have her buried in the chapel graveyard here." I went home feeling troubled, because I remembered that, years before, he had told me, that if anything happened, and Mother passed away before him, he should want to come and live with me. (I had two unmarried sisters then, and one had been with them for two or three years then, owing to Mother's ill health, and she was more than willing to keep house for him. However, he would not stay and, eventually, did as he said, and came to our house. I was very cast down, for I knew that, although my father was a godly man and had been a good father, yet his natural temperament made him very difficult to deal with sometimes, and I had suffered much in my spirit at times, when living at home with my parents before I was married. I did not say that I could have him, because my husband was away on a preaching tour in the West Country. I made the arrangements for Mother's funeral to be from Bethersden, we, who lived there, meeting the cortege from Bodle Street at Tenterden, my husband coming from where he was, to attend the Funeral Service, and then travelling back to fulfil his engagements. The rest of the family all returning to my home for a meal and, as many as possible, staying for the night. By various alterations, I made it possible for as many as could, to stay at my house, the rest going to my brother's house, until after the service held for her at our chapel the next day. The next day, before taking his breakfast, he (Father) told me what room he would like, and how I could alter this thing and the other to make room for what he wanted to have. I tried again to persuade him to remain in the nice little house they had at Bodle Street, and which we felt had been almost miraculously provided for them when they had come out of business years before.

However, my father was obdurate, and my husband, seeking to help him, as he hoped, gave consent to him coming when he came back home. In less than a fortnight, he moved and gave up his home. Beware of ever doing this, unless you are certain you are being divinely led in it. I realized that I had already more than I had strength or time to deal with and, while I was willing to do all I could for my father, I could not feel, in my heart, that my father had been as prayerful, or as careful, as I felt he should have been over such an important matter, as it had all been done so hurriedly, and I knew that there was not the necessity for it. Also, I felt very sorry for my two unmarried sisters, for they had not got a home now. The elder one was in a situation in which she had been for years and was established there, and home, for her, meant somewhere to go on her days off duty. We were too far off for that. For the younger one, my father spared enough for her to furnish a bedsitting room, as she wished to remain near the Dicker chapel, of which she had become a member. This meant, however, that she had to earn her own living in what way she could, and it was very hard going sometimes, though my father made her a little allowance. My father stayed at my house nearly three years. At times he went for a few days to stay with others of his married children, (of whom there were eight). Also, he furnished another bedsitting room at my youngest sister's house in Smarden, three miles from here, with some of his furniture. My father, during the years he was at Bodle Street, while not joining the Church there, (which we thought he would do by transfer from St. Albans), was quite a help to the friends there in carrying out the services, and he was depended on, quite a lot, by the friends there for many things which he could do. I have thought that he would have found quite a lot of consolation in being thus actively employed, even in renovations sometimes, as he was a first class carpenter and could turn his hand to many kinds of work. I have always, in my heart, felt that he made a big mistake, for, after the first novelty of getting his room right, he often seemed restless and unhappy. My husband encouraged him when he said he would like to have a typewriter, and he got one, and, after a time, he became quite able to use it, and it gave him much interest, for which I was very glad. Oh, we do need to take heed against moving without the cloud going before. Nevertheless, we did all we could to make him happy. Eight months later, after my mother's death, my daughter, Lois, was born. When I first saw her, she was like a miniature edition of my mother. During the time previous to her birth, as well as having additional anxiety in the care of my father, we had the usual anxieties and cares; which most parents have in bringing up a family. My niece was with me and was a great help. Joyce was two years and nine months old and, being of a particularly happy disposition, had settled down to altered conditions quite happily. Previously to my father's coming and before my mother's death, I had my husband's sister with us for quite a long time, who was ill with Tuberculosis. She was the one who had joined the Church by baptism at "Bethel," Luton, the year Joyce was born. When she was ill and had to leave Luton, we offered to have her, as her own home, (her parents' home), being very low-ceilinged and confined in a street, was not considered suitable for that complaint. Our house being well built, with ceiling heights higher than usual, and being surrounded on three sides by fields, away from public thoroughfares, was singularly free from dust. She remained down here, (the last part of the time with a friend), receiving treatment as an outpatient at the Clinic in Ashford, where I usually accompanied her on her visits there. The day came when she was pronounced free from symptoms, and cured, but they strongly recommended that she should not go back to the town or into the work in which she was engaged, as it required her, to inspect under a magnifying glass, every roll of ribbon which came into the wholesale shop which supplied many of the manufacturers in Luton, (a town noted for millinery). However, she would not submit. One doctor who had watched the case through, said to me: "If she goes back to that, Mrs. Dawson, the very fine dust will affect her lung again. She needs to work in open-air conditions, or, at least, where she can have air and light." In her case, she was in artificial light always, because it was too dark otherwise. I could understand quite well her desire to return to her own Place of Worship, and to be under her own pastor, but I felt she was being wilful. Then, unasked for and unlooked for, an offer was made to her, from our own local postmaster, to take up the position there of the Chief Clerk in the Post Office, in surroundings which were light and pleasant, only a very few minutes walk from our house, where we could have seen to it that she had regular meal times, and the type of nourishment most suitable for her. She almost scorned the idea of such a thing.

We were all disappointed, including our doctor, who told me that, if she went back, (and what he feared would happen, did), she would not recover the second time, explaining that, if the tissue of the lung broke down the second time, it never healed again. This is exactly what did happen, and she came back to the friend's house, hiring a room or so there, and died there after a long, suffering period. My father was then occupying the room in our house, which she had occupied. It was very sad, and I often fretted because I could not do for her, myself, what I would have gladly done. She passed away early one morning and, (as I feared it would be), entirely alone, so that we did not have what we would so have liked to have, any knowledge of her end. My husband visited her daily, and I wrote little notes to her, which sometimes she would send answers back, if she was able. (In the later part of her life, she was completely bed-ridden and her poor body was shattered with the distressing cough night and day). When my husband took me to see her, only a day or so before she died, she was too weak to speak much and I, myself, was in very poor health just then. I bent over and expressed the desire that the Lord would be with her and bless her indeed, to which she replied with pressing my hand, and giving assent to the desire expressed by movement of her head. She was too weak to speak. Then I pressed a kiss upon her forehead as warmly as I could, and said: "Goodbye, my dear, Goodbye." She struggled to speak, and then she said "Goodbye…dear," having to pause between the words and yet emphasizing the 'dear'. It meant, oh, such a lot to me, for someone had dealt very treacherously and had tried to undermine our friendship. But God was greater than man, even in that, and I was comforted. I often think of the lonely hours which she spent and I so often desired to be with her, but was not allowed to be. How good it is that God is greater than man, and that He does crown the work of our hands, and in that He did, for, when I first undertook the care of her those years before, I did it to her because she was the Lord's, and she so dreaded entering a sanatorium, because she would be cut off from the worship of God. I often think of her poor afflicted body, and how very low she was brought down, but, poor dear, we did hope and feel that she <u>did</u> enter into that "Rest that remaineth" where the inhabitants of that land shall no more say: "I am sick!" I have felt so glad that for her it was true. We found out afterwards that those two words spoken to me were her last. She never spoke again. That little episode was sacred to my husband and myself, because we knew what our desires had been for her. It was a sad trial to him to see his sister (she was the youngest one), suffer as she did, as he was greatly attached to his sisters. His other sister was the late Mrs. R. Morris, whose husband was, at one time, pastor at Clifton, in Bedfordshire. She died in early middle age, but we believe, even though she was not baptized, that she was one of the Lord's people. She left a testimony at Grove, (near Wantage), when she went home to see her mother. Our brother-in-law Mr. W. Hope, (late of Abingdon), my sister's husband, was preaching at Grove, and was led to preach from Revelation 21. 4. "And God shall wipe away all tears from their eyes;" etc., etc. This sermon was made a great help to her and, quite contrary to her usual manner, she spoke freely of it, for she was exceedingly reticent (and this was intensified because she had the impediment of a bad form of stammering). She was often thus prevented from expressing things, which at another time she could have done quite freely. She returned home to her husband and family and very, very shortly afterwards was taken severely ill and rushed into hospital. An immediate operation was performed, but the illness proved fatal. The help she received in Berkshire was, undoubtedly, her anointing for her burial. My brother-in-law, Mr. Hope, often spoke of it, and was greatly encouraged himself by this, as he had felt so strongly impressed that he must preach from it.

These side lights on our family life affected us more than would appear on the surface. In almost every instance it also affected members of our Cause, who were related either by blood relationship or marriage, and to all it is, at all times, a solemnity when those we have known and esteemed are taken from us by death. I often think of the words that came to me once, when young, on hearing of the death of one younger than myself whom I had well known: "So teach *us* to number our days, that we may apply *our* hearts unto wisdom."

Chapter 11

Now, once more, to return to our home affairs. We found much real happiness in having our children around us. Little Lois arrived, though only very slowly, and we had anxious fears, sometimes, that she would not survive early childhood, in spite of all our care. Yet I could not lose the hope that I had that she would. We named her after a friend whom we greatly esteemed (and who had passed away very early in her married life, at the birth of her child). Lois, and also Phebe, both of which names were concerning Timothy, the apostle who was taught by his mother and grandmother in the Scriptures. I remembered my own mother, who had closely followed that pattern, and we liked the names and used them.

My husband's health, at that time, was still a cause of great concern, and he was often cast down on account of it. He was often away for a few days, and I often felt anxious about him. I realized that it was the path that I was called upon to take in these frequent absences, and I felt that it would not be right of me to persuade him not to go, no matter how anxious I was, as long as he felt he could do it. The ministry of the Word of God is quite different from any other employment or calling in life. If he had been engaged in a secular calling, I would have often tried to persuade him to give up, when he was so poorly. But not in that labour! I often had this word in my mind: "know that the LORD hath set apart him that is godly for Himself." But it kept me very prayerful at times, that the Lord would strengthen him and bring him safely back. It was often a concern among the children, ranging in ages from 13 downwards, that Daddy should come home on the day we expected him. One day, one of my little ones said: "Will Daddy come home today, Mummy?" I said: "If all is well, dear." She said: "Don't say, 'If all is well', Mummy, say, 'He will'." They sometimes reminded me, if I did say that, that I had prayed with them that Daddy would be brought safely home, and, therefore, he would be sure to come. Children have wonderful faith but, like us at times, they have it tried, because, on more than one occasion, he wasn't able to come on account of his health for a day or two after. Then I had to pray for wisdom to explain to them how prayer is answered, but not always just as we expected it to be.

Things at Chapel were going on steadily. The congregation grew in numbers, little by little. Others were added to the Church, then, on the other hand, some were taken away by death, and were laid in the grave in sure and certain hope of a joyful resurrection. The Lord still continued, in His mercy, to provide for our needs, often in most remarkable ways, and, above all, He did keep alive His fear in our hearts, keeping us watching and waiting at His Throne of Grace: a very lowly, but very safe, position. We hourly, not only daily, felt to need His wisdom and grace to uphold us, day by day. When my baby, Lois, was about 15 months old, I became aware that another little one was to be added later on to our family circle.

We were, at that time, rather pressed down with many cares. Our needs were many, with our family to provide for, but often those needs gave us errands to the Throne of Grace, and the answers were often, to us, conspicuous and marked. I would like to relate here one instance for which I felt so grateful to the Lord. It covered a little need, as some would count it, but to me it was a great one. On the occasion of my having to move my baby to a cot, because the cradle was rather small, I had to move my fourth little girl out of her cot into a small bedstead. I shifted bedding around, and eventually got her new bed ready for her. She suffered much with rheumatic trouble and I liked, if possible, for her always to lay on a blanket, to help her in this. I hadn't one that I could spare to take off of a bed to lay under. When everything was tidy, I, as usual, got the little ones, who were not at school, ready to take them for a little walk. As I pushed the pram round the paths, I was still thinking of the blanket I should like to have, and I remember thinking that I wouldn't mind if it was rather thin and old. I could cut it into two, so that she always had something woollen to lay upon. As I walked by the side of the chapel, our chapel keeper in those days (Mrs. Nicholls) opened her door and called to me. She then told me she had been going through her blanket box. (She had some come to her when her father died and his home was given up). She had found some that were rather thin, which she thought I could make use of for a cot or a little bed, and she asked me if I would be offended if she gave them to me. I thought it was most wonderful, and told her what I had just been thinking, and how it would so well fill the need. She, of course, was most pleased that it was like that. I took them round to my house, and I believe that both she, who gave them, and I, who received them, felt our hearts warmed and cheered, and my little daughter did not have to sleep, even one night, without the blanket to lay on. Ours, for many years, was indeed a hand basket portion, as regards providential things. On no occasion were we allowed to have anything in hand.

At the time Miriam, our ninth child, was expected, I developed bronchitis and was very ill for a time, then, as I got up and about again, influenza came upon each in the house. I remember feeling so burdened, as my father and all were ill. But the Lord healed them each, quickly. I remember on one Saturday, as I tried to straighten things up for Sunday, that I cried as I went round, as I could not get ease anywhere. When my patients were all about again, my doctor came to see me and told me that I must have my nurse in, and that I must rest, almost entirely, till baby's birth. Two or three weeks before she was born, my husband (and my father) went to Oxford for him to baptize the second son of Mr. and Mrs. W. Hope, who, at that time, lived in Oxford, and were members of that church, before Mr. Hope's call to the pastorate at Abingdon. While they were away, my husband had a peculiarly deep exercise of mind concerning the baby to be born, and was even given the name of the child. I had one too, in thinking of her, that I did hope that she would be the subject of grace, and I had also thought much about Miriam's 'Song of Deliverance,' and Miriam was the name I wanted her to have, especially as I had lost a cousin Miriam, whom I had always much liked. When my husband came home and we were alone, I said to him: "I have thought of some names for our baby, dear, and it is evident it is to be a girl, because I think the name was given to me." He said, "Don't say any more. I will tell you what her name is to be – Grace Miriam." It was wonderful that we both felt that, whatever life held in store for her, and whether or not we should be allowed to keep her, that she would be made manifest as a child of God.

One day, my husband left home, going straight on from where he was preaching in the evening, (either Grafty Green or Hawkhurst) to London, to stay at my sister's house there, to go down to Hook Norton the following morning, for Special Services on the Monday afternoon and evening, it being Whitsuntide weekend. He had not been at all well and I felt, inwardly, as I wished him 'Goodbye,' and saw him go across the lawn, that he should not go, but remain at home, for he looked so very poorly. As I have stated before, if it had been any other work than the work of the ministry, I should have strongly urged him to stay at home, but I felt I must not try to stop him from that work. (Minister's wives have a peculiar pathway to walk in that way, and very few people know how much it costs to try to put their own feelings on one side, especially is this the case in the lives of those whose husbands travel widely for weekday services, too, as they are wholly in the ministry.)

He went to Hook Norton and was enabled to go through the services. He was greatly helped and others were helped also, some of them in a marked way, in hearing.

The next day, we were expecting him, and were eagerly looking forward to resuming our normal home life again. I still felt weak, but was desirous now to take up the reins of housekeeping and, with the help of Ruth, my eldest daughter, to do the work entailed. I had almost finished the washing when a telegram arrived. "Too unwell to travel home – Writing." As I was still weak and had also got very tired in doing the work, it took hold of me rather, physically, apart from the great disappointment I felt, and I knew the children would feel, too, and also, I was terribly anxious, because I remembered how he looked when he left home on the Sunday, and this was Tuesday morning, or rather, just about noontide. I went indoors, through to my dining-room and shut the door. I sat down and picked up the Bible, and asked the Lord to lead me to some word of His which would give me some hope concerning this, and also direction. I opened the Bible on this word; unknown to me before: "and Jacob shall return, and be in rest." It seemed to be a promise of his return home and that gave me a little courage concerning the future. I had my nine children all at home with me...the eldest, Ruth, was about 14½ years, and my baby was about seven or eight weeks old. I tried to ask the Lord to give me quietness of mind, and grace to meet the various needs as they arose. The letter arrived the next day to tell me that the doctor had diagnosed Mr. Dawson's illness as phlebitis, and that it would necessitate him resting completely, for the time being. It so happened that his hostess, the eldest daughter of the deacon of the Cause, who was a widower, was a fully trained nurse, and there were two sons, too, who could give aid if necessary, in helping to nurse him. It was an acute attack of this trouble, and he suffered quite a lot of pain. My husband and I corresponded daily, as letters came almost daily for him, some of which I could reply to on his behalf at once, and others he could answer from his sick room, or could write me to tell me how to reply. Also, in our personal letters to each other, we could and did encourage ourselves, and each other, in God. Here I will relate an experience which I had, which was a most salutary lesson, and which I have never forgotten. We had, as almost everyone who is interested in the things of God has, a daily text calendar. I had tried, for my children's sake, and for the sake of others around me, to keep a very calm exterior over my trouble, and, while I felt it ever so keenly, and feared greatly at times, I never expressed it to anyone. At times, however, when by myself, I was terribly tried as to whether I should ever have him back home again, but I did constantly ask for grace to be calm and quiet, but I had been told that my father, deceived by my exterior attitude, had said that he didn't think that I realized what a serious state my husband was in, and what the issue might be. One of my sisters-in-law said she thought I did. The reaction upon me, though I said nothing, was to make me feel very, very cast down, and I did what was very unwise, and tried to probe into the near future by looking ahead into the text calendar. (This was on Sunday evening). The text for Monday was: "Blessed *are* the dead which die in the Lord....: Yea, saith the Spirit, that they may rest from their labours: and their works do follow them." My feelings cannot be described. It was a great shock, but I thought I would look further. The next one for Tuesday was concerning, "Ye sorrow not, even as others which have no hope," and the next one, concerning burial. I could not describe to anyone how I felt. Now, in the house next door to us were living three maiden ladies whose sister was the wife of Mr. James Sharples, the pastor, then, of "Evington" Chapel, near Leicester. She and her husband and daughter had come a week or so before to stay with the Misses Paffard, as Mrs. Sharples was in a very poor state of health. Actually, she was suffering with cancer, and, at the time they came to Bethersden, her condition worsened greatly, so much so, that she was never able to return to "Evington" and, of course, her husband and daughter stayed, too. She was very ill on the Sunday when I looked at the texts, but I didn't think of her. I thought only of my sick husband and dreaded what news I might have. I kept all this to myself because of my children. Mrs. Sharples died on the Monday evening, so that one text was most applicable for our bereaved friends in the next house, and so were the others too.

Previously, however, to that happening, I had been pondering over it during the night, and I thought, all at once – 'I expect that hundreds of people have that calendar up in their homes. They will each read that text for tomorrow, and it could not possibly be that that particular text could be applicable to each of them, and is there any reason that it is particularly for me?' Besides, I had tried to probe into the future. There is no Scriptural warrant for that, and I felt guilty. Also, on the Monday I had a letter from Hook Norton telling me that my husband was a little better, so if I had quietly rested upon the promise that I hope God did give to me, (when in the first place I had asked Him to guide me to some word of His, upon which my mind should be stayed), "Jacob shall return, and be in rest," I would have been saved many hours of sorrowful apprehension as regards what would be. It was a lesson I have not forgotten. We must rest upon the promise God hath spoken, in all things ordered well for us. We have His divine warrant to rest upon that, but not upon anything less. (This occurred a week or so after the Anniversary.) The Anniversary Services were held, and my husband's doctor had written a short statement, which was read to the congregation, concerning how he was.

During the time that he was away, (which included six Sundays), ministers kindly helped by preaching in the afternoon or, once, all day, and we were helped through this time of trial. Prayer Meetings or Reading Services were held when no minister was available, and weekly Prayer Meetings were held. There was, of course, the daily watching the Lord's hand, that is, for our daily needs. We had then nine children, and our needs, however simply we lived, were many. But the Lord was good. In many ways those needs were supplied, sometimes, indeed often, in kind. Our garden was a help, as things my husband had sowed and planted began to yield some supplies, and nothing we really needed was lacking. During that time, our children were maintained in health. I, myself, grew stronger and, after the Lord restored to me the peace I lost when I tried to look ahead, which He kindly did very soon, I was enabled to go on day by day, hoping against hope, often feelingly sinking, yet enabled to swim. The Word of God says: "They that trust in the LORD *shall be* as mount Zion, *which* cannot be removed, *but* abideth for ever." I often feared that I could not be amongst these favoured people, because I so often seemed moved in my feelings, hopes and fears alternating, but I always came back to myself like this. 'Well, I do hope in the Lord, I have no other hope, and no other help.'

The happy time came, at last, for my husband's return. He was much better, but by no means really well. But it was a real joy to have him back home, and I felt a real burden lifted off my shoulders, because I had him at my side, whatever eventuality arose, to consult, and to share it with me. It was many weeks before he really regained strength, but he persevered with the treatment our doctor advised. At first, he could only preach once on a Sunday and, except for walking round the garden about twice in the day and, sitting occasionally for a meal, he laid on the sofa in his Study, where he did much writing and, also, searching of the Word of God, so that his mind should be well furnished for when he could go forth once more to his labours in the Lord's vineyard, which thing did come about, through God's goodness, toward the end of the year. On August Bank Holiday Monday of that year, as usual for that day, he was engaged to give a children's address and to preach in the evening at Bounds Cross chapel, Biddenden. Arrangements had been made, so that we could all go, and I could not say how eagerly I looked forward to that, as I had had many months without going further than a walk in the village. In the morning of that day he conducted, at our chapel, the Wedding Service for our niece, who had lived with us for so long, and our deacon's son. It was a very happy and right union and my husband was pleased to do it. However, after the service he felt ill, (he had preached twice the day before), and found he would not be strong enough to go to Biddenden after all. Some friends arranged it so that the older children were not disappointed, and so seven of them went, and I had the two youngest with me. My husband had gone to bed. (He himself was very disappointed, especially as he had to disappoint the friends who would have been, and were, there.) I saw my older children off from our gate, and then returned indoors. As I pushed my baby's pram indoors, I went into my husband's Study, and I remember saying: "Why is it, Lord, that things seem so constantly to work against me?" It seemed such a lawful thing to desire and to do, to all go out to a neighbouring chapel, and to have somewhere where our older children could go and, very lawfully, spend the Bank Holiday.

I felt almost rebellious, though I did not want to be a rebel. God knew my heart in that, but, self-pity did seem as though it would gain the mastery, but it did not do so, for the Lord spoke, so very kindly, this to my heart: "Have I been a wilderness unto Israel?" Oh, I was right melted down, and I answered aloud, as I was in the room by myself: "No, Lord. Thou hast never been that! Thou hast been to me all that Thou didst promise to be!" I felt, oh, so full of love and gratitude, and yet shame that I felt I could not get low enough, nor give unto the Lord the praise that was due to Him. I truly felt He was my Father and I was His child, and He had comforted me! I went upstairs and saw my husband, and we were able to converse on the things of God, and even though he was so spent and poorly, I had got the pleasure of him being back home again, and not ill away from me, as he had been, and God had confirmed me in the knowledge that I was His child, and that he was my God, so it was a good day, even though there was disappointment at first. During my husband's long time of ill health, from the time of his first being laid aside at Hook Norton, the Lord was pleased to give us many tokens of His care for us. Many people, from different parts of the country to whom we had to write to cancel engagements, were constrained to send some token of their esteem for my husband's ministry. Some of it came here, and some of it went to him at Hook Norton when he was there. The chapel people remembered him in a practical way, by still putting money into the pastor's fund. My husband told them, as usual, to pay the supplying ministers out of this, the rest was brought in to me. When my husband returned home and we had been favoured to meet all our expenses fully, we found he had just a few pounds left. He said he didn't want his portion here, but it was ordered, that the little he had in hand was enough to supplement our expenses until he was well enough to go out again for week evenings and Sunday evening services. Thus we again proved He was faithful who had promised to supply all our need. We went through the next year finding our pathway to be one of 'ups and downs,' but we still proved that there were quite as many 'ups' as 'downs', though (as I think it was Bunyan who wrote) "the Christian man is seldom long at ease, before one trial's o'er another doth him seize." We must speak of deliverance as well as trials. We must speak of relief as well as griefs and cares. Clouds are balanced. We would not be able to abundantly utter the memory of the great goodness if we did not speak, also, of the background of the way we had to take, sometimes beside the still waters. Also, if we would desire to be (as we so often did) followers of them who, through faith and patience, inherited the promises, we must expect, also, in our little measure, to walk in the pathway that they had to walk in. It is only a small measure to what those in Scriptural days, (as we read in Hebrews 11 & 12), and others since, have had to walk. We have been spared many trials and extremities of suffering, which they had to endure. (I personally wonder how I would be able to endure if I had such trouble and sufferings. Only on one basis: "Thy grace sufficed saints of old; It made them strong and made them bold, And it suffices still." "Still is He gracious, wise, and just, And still in Him let Israel trust.")

When Miriam was two years old, Christine was born. She is the last one of our family (living). We named Christine after the second wife of my brother, who died when her second baby was due, and who died in the Lord, and who praised and blessed Him as she died. I, as usual, was very poorly before her birth, as my heart condition made itself more apparent under those circumstances. I had to rest as much as was possible. My two elder girls, Ruth and Bertha, were very helpful with the younger children, and we were a very happy family, even though we had to work hard, and do much contriving to make ends meet. The Lord was with us, but He still taught us that we must fix our whole dependence upon Him. It meant daily, and almost hourly, prayer for grace, wisdom and strength. So often this verse came to my mind:

> "Thy whole dependence on Me fix;
> Nor entertain a thought
> Thy worthless schemes with Mine to mix,
> But venture to be nought."

I think I must have needed much teaching of that lesson, for the Lord so often seemed, in His dealings with us in our circumstances, to shut me up to Himself, so that I had to work and walk that out. But, I say this to His honour, He never failed me, even though I sometimes thought that perhaps I could scheme a way out. When I, at last, asked Him for wisdom to deal with these needs and problems, He so kindly gave it. Wisdom to deal with the everyday cares, often noticeably being given when the children needed fresh garments, by giving wisdom to know how to use something I had by me, when I had no money that could be spared for new garments. There was quite a sweet pleasure in working in this way, especially when, sometimes, one felt that the Lord did indeed condescend to attend to one's wants and needs, even in this way. I am sure I have felt quite as much gratitude, and even more, than some have felt when they could go into a shop with sufficient money in hand to buy new garments for their children. Sometimes, a piece of cloth or material remnants have been sent, I have laid them out on the large table and looked at each piece, and then have prayed for wisdom as to how they could be used. Even small things then are really precious, if one could feel in one's heart they were the Lord's provision. The lonely hours when my husband was away in the week, fulfilling engagements were thus occupied, and spent in our house, which was a nice roomy one. I felt we were all where he would like to feel we were, and, often, I could join in with the children's pleasures, even while I worked. For many years, I never left my children, if my husband was away, but I never got tired of their company. In warmer weather and long days, I found quite a little work in our large garden, which I and the children enjoyed. I wanted, from my heart, to be willing for my husband to be fully employed in his work in the ministry. My husband often tried to encourage me, by quoting to me; "As is his part that goeth forth to the battle, so is her part that abideth at home by the stuff." I think I can say, without being egotistical, that I did sometimes feel that the Lord was giving me that part that was mine, in the quietness of mind and contentment with the lot He had obtained for me, which, at times, I was favoured with. I know of no better way to combat loneliness or perplexity, than by taking it to the Lord in prayer, and then looking around to see what needs to be done, and to do that willingly and cheerfully, even if it is only the daily round and common task. Those whom I had to live with me for helps, willingly entered into the routine we followed. Gradually, we got quite into the habit of doing the extra things, in my husband's absence, such as chimneys to be swept, blankets, quilts and curtains to be washed, furniture to be polished, and upholstery cleaned etc. Cupboards had to be turned out, all of which excitements kept the children amused and entertained while we did it, and our minds occupied with working out the details, so that, when he was at home, the usual everyday routine could be quietly followed, at least, as quietly as a household of children and young people could be quiet. I am very, very glad to find that each of our children look back upon their childhood as a very happy one. There were so many things I would have liked to do for them, and I often inwardly grieved because I could not do them, but they did not miss them nearly as much as I feared they would do, when they saw others having things which we could not get for them. I am sure, now, that it was good for them to have to learn to do without some things, which, while lawful in themselves, we were not in a position to obtain for them. It gave them initiative to make their own games and pleasures with what was obtainable, and to be satisfied with what they had got.

I was very poorly while my baby was coming, as my constant heart weakness became more apparent as I got older. About this time, our old doctor retired at an advanced age, and a complete stranger took his practice. The first time I had occasion to see him (my two older sisters had wanted to do so. They were staying a few days with me, and were concerned about my health), he examined my heart, and then said: "You must go to bed for at least six weeks." I was dismayed and I said: "But I can't do that, Doctor, I haven't anyone to do my housekeeping for me." He replied: "I am your doctor, and I say you must." I replied: "I will promise you to rest upon every possible occasion, and I will do everything I can do sitting, and not standing." I said: "There is just one more probability, Doctor, but I am not sure about it yet, (owing to my age, and also an infirmity I have, I cannot say for certain), but I may be pregnant." He said: "I sincerely hope not." I replied: "Why, Doctor, I have children." He exclaimed: "What!" "Yes," I said, "I have nine children." He replied: "Well, I can hardly believe it, for I would have said, had I been asked, that it was a physical impossibility for you to have a child at all." I have just mentioned this for any person who should read this in the future to see what God can do, and does do, for those who trust in Him; always remembering faith (true faith) is the gift of God, not anything that we can produce, or enact, at our will. But, if one is desirous of doing His will, as far as walking in His ways in our lives, He will honour the faith He gives. So, once more, I proved the truth of what God had promised to me, and my baby (Christine) was born, and while the doctor was in charge of the case. He did not come for some hours after we sent for him, because he said he was engaged, which is very probable in a country practice, where their patients live so many miles away from the doctor's house.

He arrived, just as she was born, and as the person with me was not a registered nurse, she had to wait a certain time before she must do anything (if the doctor was not there at the actual birth). He did arrive in time to do what was required of him. He was very evidently quite unused to that part of a doctor's work. He had been, for many years, an army doctor and, as it proved, he himself suffered with severe heart weakness. He was glad for Miss. Pay to help him, and he was glad that I was brought through safely, because, quite evidently, he had been afraid I would not be. He was kind and as efficient as he knew how to be, afterwards. Very shortly afterwards he died, very suddenly, in his home. Once more, however, God proved Himself to be a very present help in trouble.

Chapter 12

At the present time (March 2nd 1965) each of our ten children are spared to us, and our youngest one is almost 32 years old. We desire to place on record God's goodness to us in this way, and we desire, (that as we have been able to take courage at times

The Dawson Family 1933

David   Ruth   Baby Christine   Elsie   Herbert
         Mercy   Lois   Joyce   Janet   Bertha   Peter
                                                   Miriam

concerning each one), that they may all be favoured to be amongst the redeemed of the Lord: "Called.... according to His own purpose," and that, if His holy will, eventually each one may be made manifest as a child of God.

We had the usual epidemics of children's complaints visit our house, as most parents do. Measles, mumps, whooping cough, German measles, chickenpox, etc. My husband's health was very poor at this period. I often felt anxious, for he was very low. I also, at this time, had my eldest daughter very, very poorly. It was on a Saturday. My husband had to spend most of his time lying on a couch on the lawn. He was too weak to do anything. Ruth's temperature, when I took it, was 105F. It startled me, and I felt anxious. I spoke to my husband about it, and asked him if I ought to phone the doctor, who lived in a neighbouring village. He had a surgery and visited Bethersden three times weekly, but, of course, came out if necessary on other days. I went and phoned, and Doctor came out and saw Ruth and my husband, too, and prescribed for each. As Ruth was laid up, I hadn't her aid, but Bertha and David did their best, and the other little ones, too. When Doctor had gone, and I had got my patients settled again, and my baby settled, I thought of the baking and cooking which had to be done. We did not have an electric cooker then and, for a big cooking, I had to have the kitchener going. I went down the garden to the shed to get some wood for lighting it. It was a very warm day in June, and I was feeling rather breathless. As I came out of the door of the shed and turned to go up the path to the back door, I turned quickly, and went momentarily faint, a very usual thing with me; especially in warm weather. I fell heavily, flat on to my face, even bruising my face as I fell, and, as it proved later, I damaged something internally. I pulled myself up, and felt cross with myself that I had not gone more steadily, and then went on with my work. The same day, in the late afternoon, feeling rather poorly on account of the heat, I had to go to the phone at our friend's house. I felt very spent out, but thought it was the result of anxiety, heat and working, and took no further thought about possible damage by the fall. But events proved that I had damaged myself. The immediate result was haemorrhage, which continued for three or four months.

It proved to be a large internal tumour, which eventually came away. I was exceedingly ill, and was being prepared for hospital. My husband was in the Study trying to pray for me, as Doctor had told him how very ill I was, and had asked him to go upstairs and ask me if I would be willing to go to hospital, as Doctor had told him that, humanly speaking, it was the only chance for my survival. My husband replied: "Well, Doctor, you do the very best you can, and we will do what you feel is best, but there is one more Physician, Doctor, and I will try to pray to Him." I had said I would go to hospital, though I felt sure I should not survive the journey. I did not tell my husband that, for I felt I must use all the means possible. When he was gone down again, and Nurse was preparing me, I was in the most severe pain. I didn't remember ever having such severe pain in my life. As I lay there, all at once this came to me with some weight: "Strengthen thee out of Zion." (I had a fear that, when the ambulance came and they began to move me, I should cry out in pain. My children were in their beds, and I feared it would distress and frighten them.) So I felt that text was for that contingency. However, after a time, this came too: "Fulfil all thy petitions." It gave me a little hope that, after all, I might recover, because there had been so many petitions that had arisen concerning our Place of Worship, and what we hoped to see done in connection with it, as to the outcome of prayer for my husband and the fruit of his labours.

So many things, which I had felt I should see done there, were as yet not evident. Then this followed: "Send thee help from the sanctuary." This is not just in the order in which they are written, but how they came to me in my great extremity. In any case, they strengthened hope within me that I should yet be brought through. Doctor came again to the bedside to help Nurse, and I heard him say: "We'll wait, Nurse. She may not have to go, there is something happening here." He said to me: "Oh, Mrs. Dawson, you must have been through a gruelling time, though you have kept so quiet." (You see, the Lord did send me help from the sanctuary.) My husband told me afterwards that he (the doctor) ran downstairs into the Study, and said: "Oh, Mr. Dawson, a miracle has happened. Mrs. Dawson may not have to go to hospital after all. It is most wonderful. I have told them to wait another hour." He came back upstairs, into my room and then, within that half hour of most agonizing pain, a large tumour, weighing six or seven pounds, came away. Of course, afterwards, I was completely exhausted, and so ill that it was feared then that I could not recover, but, though I couldn't say so, I felt I should come through. For two or three days Doctor came three times a day, and he even came on the Sunday morning before he went to Church, as he felt he might be sent for. But, the Lord was with us and, though I was most critically ill, yet He did restore me, after many weeks, to a measure of health and strength. It was the second week in December before I was able to begin to be more active, though still in bed. I had, for quite a little while, been favoured in reading the Word of God with His blessing, and a felt sense of nearness to Him in prayer. But, one day this came to my heart very powerfully: "Enter into His gates with thanksgiving, *and* into His courts with praise: be thankful unto Him, *and* bless His name." I thought it over, and I could only conclude that it meant literally what it said, and that I should get up, and once more go into Chapel to praise God for me. At the same time, I felt that I should suffer spiritually if I did not. I mentioned to the doctor that I would like to try to get up now. He replied that I must on no account do so, as he did not know just what would happen if I tried to get up and put my feet to the ground. I had not been off the bed since the night in October when the tumour passed from me. I said that I really did feel that I must try, but he was adamant about it, and said he would not give his consent. After he had gone, I took the matter to the Lord in prayer. He knew that I did desire to obey the command He had laid upon me. The next time I tried with no better success with my doctor. He was coming in once more on the Friday, and I did pray, most earnestly, that the Lord would so move his heart that he would consent to me sitting out of bed. I again asked him, and I said to him: "Doctor, I shall have to get up now. I am quite sure of this, I shall make no further progress now until I do." He said: "Do you really feel that?" I said: "Yes, Doctor. Don't be afraid to let me try. I feel sure it will be alright." "Well," he said, "you people are different from any other people I know, I can't understand it." (He knew some of our members who were his patients, one or two of them elderly and very poorly in health.) Finally, after much hesitation, he consented to my request that I might sit in a chair by the side of the bed. That was the token which I had asked of the Lord, so that I could know I was not presuming, but only obeying His voice. I sat out after dinner-time, and had my tea later on. I felt, as I expected to feel, very weak and ill, but I still felt quite sure that I must go forward to obey the command given: "Enter into His gates with thanksgiving, *and* into His courts with praise:" It was now Friday evening, and I felt convinced that I must go out to Chapel on Sunday. I thought that I must now try to walk, so I held on to the bedstead, and managed to just get round to the other side. While there, leaning on a chest of drawers for support, I felt so ill that I feared I should die before I could get back to bed, and I was, oh, so confused. I felt that, after all, I should prove I had been presumptuous, and that it was not faith, true faith, at all, when this came, spoken into my heart with power: "Covenant purposes" – "A time to be born, and a time to die." I immediately answered: "Yes, Lord, and if I stay in bed for the rest of my life, I shall not add one hour to it, and if I get up and obey the command Thou hast given me, I shall not lessen it by a single hour," and how strengthened I then felt in my heart. I knew then that it was not acting presumptuously to be obedient to the command given to me. I managed to get back into my chair, feeling already strengthened. That was Friday evening. On Saturday, in the early afternoon, I went downstairs. Sitting down, I managed to do a few things to help my girls, who had all rallied round me to do all they could to help me, and their father and the other children. It was wonderful what they managed to do, and I did feel so thankful that they had been enabled to do it. On Sunday afternoon I went to Chapel. Everyone who saw me was startled by my appearance (I learned afterwards) but I had no thought of that. My one thought was, I had been enabled to do what I had been bidden to do – "Enter into His gates with thanksgiving, *and* into His courts with praise: be thankful unto Him, and bless His name." I no longer felt that I was at a distance from Him, or that He was distant from me. In those days of extreme weakness and trial, I was very sensitive in my soul's feelings. The Lord Jesus Christ was to me a 'living bright reality.' I longed, always, to feel that He was near to me. (Writing this, years afterwards, I have known what it is to feel that it was with me as in times past, when the candle of the Lord shone round my head.) As one remembers the afflictions in which one had to walk; relative and personal illness, severe pain and weakness, anxiety and poverty, there is a very natural shrinking of one's flesh from having to walk in a similar path, to obtain spiritual blessings of like manner to those that I had enjoyed before.

The Lord knows our needs from day to day, and from year to year. I have often, since these many different experiences which I have had, felt to be in full agreement with the hymnwriter, when he said:

"Under Thy forming hands, my God,
Give me that frame which Thou lik'st best."

I have proved, in my long life, that the nature of the trials differ widely, so that yesterday's supply of grace would not meet the nature of the trial that is appointed for me today or tomorrow. I used, as a child, to ponder over what I used to hear different ones ask for at a Prayer Meeting – fresh supplies of grace. It is so necessary! The Israelites had to gather manna daily, didn't they? And so we have to be daily made to feel ourselves undone, that we might be kept dependent upon Him.

After this time of trial, we went on for a time quite quietly, but I did not get as strong as I should have done. Then, in about a year's time, it was confirmed that I should have another baby in May. Before that came to pass, however, I was very ill with bronchitis and pneumonia, following on influenza with which we were all ill. Once again, the Lord appeared for me and I was restored from illness. I had been thinking upon the case of Peter's wife's mother, and how we read that Jesus touched her hand and the fever left her, and she arose and ministered unto them. I felt then that He still had powers to heal me even now. The family were downstairs, having just had breakfast and family worship, when my eldest brother, Mr. Percy Aldworth, (who at that time was living in the village) came into the house, and said: "I have been reading this morning about Peter's wife's mother being sick of a fever, and how Jesus touched her hand and the fever left her. Now," he said, "I feel that God is able to do the same for Elsie and that she will be raised up again." I began to gain strength, up to a point, and was over that particular illness enough, that when it came to my little Caleb's birth, I was brought safely through myself, but my little one's soul was taken from the womb to heaven. I am sure of that, because I had such a spirit of prayer given to me for him. I asked them to leave him by me, so that I might look on him for a little while. His little face was as full of happiness as it could be, and I was sure that it was registered in his face as the peace of God. When later on I was able to go to Chapel, a dear old lady (who was in the district for a little while) was there. She came to me after the service, and said: "Oh, Mrs. Dawson, don't think that you have come through all this for nothing." I said: "I don't, Mrs. Stevens." "No," she said: "I am quite sure your baby is in heaven, to praise God there." I replied that I had been comforted by that very feeling myself. I was sure that he was there. I felt quite a sense of personal loss and bereavement at the time, because, whenever I was led to pray for my unborn child, I always referred to it as "him" and "he," for I felt quite assured in my mind that it would be a boy, and his name was given to me once in Chapel, when my husband was preaching and referred to Caleb as one "who followed the Lord fully." It appealed to me greatly, and as I felt sure I should have a son on this occasion, I registered it in my mind as the name for him. I did not think, then, of how my many prayers on his behalf would be answered, by him being taken to heaven to serve the Lord fully there. His little, untenanted body was buried in our local

Churchyard, and is there awaiting the resurrection morning. Afterwards, I steadily gained strength, and was able to resume my normal life as a housewife and mother. We went on then, for a time, fairly quietly. The next thing to be recorded is the death of my godly father. He, only too evidently, had a stroke one week, and died a few days afterwards. He recovered consciousness quickly when he was first taken ill, but his speech was affected, very evidently, and he was unable ever to get up again. He was taken much worse on the Good Friday morning. My husband was due to preach at Crowborough. He took me to my sister's home at Smarden, where my father was, and took two or three of the family with him. Ruth had been married not long previously, and she and her husband were taking care of the younger ones. He, my father, lingered longer than we had thought he might do. Some of us were not able to stay all the while. When my husband returned from Crowborough, he called for me to take me home, as one of my little girls who had gone with me, had been taken rather poorly. Those of my father's family who were able to stay, spoke of what a profitable time they had in listening to what he had spoken during the night. He remained in much the same state of health; sleeping or partly unconscious. When conscious, it was evident that he was fully able to grasp things, though not always able to reply, as his speech was so affected. On Sunday morning, when I went over, it was evident that he was sinking. We watched him until about 4.00 pm, when he gently ceased breathing, and thus passed quietly and peacefully to his eternal rest.

> "How blessed the righteous when he dies,
> As sinks the weary soul to rest."

To some, the word "rest" seems to have a greater significance than to others. Some, like my father, know, for the greater part of their life, what toil, both mental and physical, meant, especially as he had been orphaned very early in his life, and had to meet the hardships of life alone, when still quite young. My mother, when he was at length married, proved to be a most suitable companion, and a real help meet for him. A godly parentage, with godly fear on both sides of the marital union, is indeed a great heritage.

CONSIDER HIM

For consider HIM that endured
such contradiction of sinners
against Himself, lest ye be
wearied and faint in your minds.
Hebrews 12. 3.

Lord, help us to consider Thee,-
Thou lovely Lamb of Calvary;
Thy lowly birth, Thy holy life;
Thine anguish, and Thy bitter strife
In lonely dark Gethsemane;
Thy sufferings upon the tree;
Thy victory over death's dark hour;
Thy glorious resurrection power;
Thy tender pity, and Thy love,
Now, as our great High Priest above;
Thy kingly state, and majesty;-
We would adore, and worship Thee.

Elsie J. Dawson

"They shall abundantly utter the memory of Thy great goodness, and shall sing of Thy righteousness." Psalm 145.7.

"He is faithful that promised." Hebrews 10.23.

"Tell *it* to the generation following." Psalm 48.13.

> "Shall the wonders God has wrought
> Be lost in silence or forgot?"

PART II

HERBERT DAWSON (1890 – 1969)
Chapter 1
CALL BY GRACE

In writing an outline of my call by grace and to preach the everlasting gospel, I feel my need of the gracious aid of the Holy Spirit as a Remembrancer, that I may be enabled to remember the way the Lord has led me. I feel it is a solemn matter to give a reason of the hope within me, remembering our hymnwriter's words:

> "Never, never may we dare,
> What we're not to say we are."

According to my own experience, I must own that I have been very cast down at times, and much tried as to whether I have been called by grace, or not, and when darkness of mind has caused past Ebenezers to be out of sight, and all one's evidences are dimmed, it leads to much searching of heart concerning one's call. I must own, also, there have been times in my experience when I have been enabled to rejoice in hope, and feel, to my joy and peace, the good work *was* begun within, and would be brought to a blessed finish.

In looking back upon my early years, and thinking upon the ungodly life I lived, and the conduct and conversation I indulged in, I can feelingly echo the psalmist's prayer: "Remember not the sins of my youth, nor my transgressions: according to Thy mercy remember Thou me for Thy goodness' sake, O LORD." Psalm 25.7

I was born at Grove, near Wantage, Berkshire, on 27th August, 1890. I gave abundant evidence, as I grew up during my school days, of what I was by nature, and, although under strict parental discipline, I frequently evaded this, and followed after the things of the flesh as opportunities arose. Upon arriving in my 'teens', I was apprenticed to the printing trade, in an office at Wantage where my parents lived. This brought me into contact with ungodly companions, and I soon began to go with them in their

153

pursuits, and became one of them in conduct, and my conversation was like theirs, often accompanied by oaths and curses. As I went on, I became much entangled with the world and the things of it, and look back, with shame, upon some of the spots and places I was found in. I can enter into the hymnwriter's feelings:

> "Preserved in Jesus when
> My feet made haste to hell;
> And there should I have gone,
> But Thou dost all things well;
> Thy love was great, Thy mercy free,
> Which from the pit delivered me."

I was much taken up with football, and billiards playing, and other games, and spent much of my leisure time in indulging in these, and when not thus occupied, I wasted many valuable hours in novel reading. So I spent five or six years of my youth. On Sunday mornings, I attended our Cause at Grove with my father, and at other times, "Zion" Chapel, Wantage, but I hated the truths that were proclaimed at both places, and made up my mind that, as soon as I could do as I liked, I should have no more to do with either Place of Worship, or the people who worshipped therein. I remember many of the faithful men of God who stood up in those pulpits, but none of their words did I heed, and the most welcome word of all was the "Amen" that concluded the service. I remember, with shame, how I used to endeavour to while away the time by dwelling upon the sinful pleasures of the previous week, or else anticipating those in the week to come. Such has been the vivid imagination of my mind that, while the preacher has been proclaiming the gospel, I have been playing a game of football over again, or recalling some other event pleasing to the carnal mind. I had no ear for the gospel trumpet, nor can I remember one text that I heard any minister preach from, until I was blessed with the hearing ear.

At length, the time came that God had designed, in His eternal purposes, for another prodigal to come to himself. Soon after I was 18 years of age, I went to play football at a little village called Stanford-in-the-Vale, on Boxing Day, 1908. I remember my mother begging me not to go, but I was determined so to do, little realizing what the outcome would be. While the game was in progress, I was injured by another player coming into collision with me, and I received a severe blow on the head, and had to be assisted off the field. I suffered much at the time, but the pain in my head was nothing to the solemnity of mind that came upon me. A solemn consciousness of what I was as a sinner, took possession of me, and my conscience was loaded with guilt. The ungodliness of my life was arrayed before me, and while no word was spoken, I felt the all-seeing eye of God search me through and through; I can only liken it to Paul's declaration: "Moreover the law entered, that the offence might abound." Truly, my offences did abound in my conscience, until I felt I must be cut off, as our hymnwriter declares:

> "Should sudden vengeance seize my breath,
> I must pronounce Thee just in death;
> And if my soul were sent to hell,
> Thy righteous law approves it well."

I returned home feeling I was a hell-deserving sinner, and with a load of misery upon my spirits I cannot describe. I entered into the publican's feelings, and how his prayer suited me: "God be merciful to me a sinner," but my fear was: "Would God be merciful to a sinner like me?"

The solemn feeling I was the subject of, produced an aching void within, which cut me off from the life I had been living, and I was enabled to turn my back upon my ungodly companions, and could no more join them on the football field, or at the club around the billiard table. Two things were made very real to me at this time: (1) the unsatisfying nature of the so-called pleasures I had indulged in all my youth, and hours spent in the devil's service, and (2) the unspeakable importance of possessing a saving knowledge of the Truth I had hitherto hated, and the favours of that God who was the sum and substance of it. From this memorable Boxing Day onwards, the Lord favoured me with grace to sever my connections with my former pursuits and pleasures, and He enabled me to join with Moses: "Choosing rather to suffer affliction with the people of God, than to enjoy the pleasures of sin for a season." I arose from my bed on that Boxing Day a sinner, dead in sin, and counting it a pleasure to fulfil the lusts of the flesh and desires of the mind; I laid down on my bed at night a sinner, alive to what I was before God – a guilty sinner.

With the change within came a change without, and now I began to go up to the house of the Lord with a purpose, and to hear what God the Lord would speak to my comfort, if so be that He would be gracious to me. I felt disappointed when the "Amen" came (as it often did) without any particular blessing for me. I went to *hear*, and to hear for myself, and I can say that my feelings regarding God's house were altogether altered, and I felt, with the psalmist: "I had rather be a door-keeper in the house of my God, than to dwell in the tents of wickedness." I felt the unspeakable importance of my soul's salvation, and my need of a manifested interest in being among that number for whom Jesus died on Calvary. Much that I heard in the ministry was, either, too deep, or too high, for me to enter into, and I used to feel cast down on account of this. Many miles did I travel around my home in the fields, pondering over my case, and begging that I might have a real religion, and be numbered with God's people. I went on for some time, and was encouraged "here a little, and there a little", sometimes by a hymn, and now and again a word dropped from the pulpit. As yet I had no 'word' that I could speak of as a word of comfort, I had 'touches,' as it were, but I wanted more. As I was thus exercised and concerned, one day, on returning to my work at midday, God was pleased to grant my desire. I had been pleading: "Lord, do make it manifest I am born again; 'Shew me a token for good'"; and the answer came with sweet confirmation: "And you *hath He quickened,* who were dead in trespasses and sins." I went on, after this 'token for good,' with a hope in God's mercy, but I still wanted the most desirable of all mercies – the knowledge of sins forgiven. I was encouraged often, to wait upon the Lord for this, and to hope the day would dawn when the Sun of Righteousness would arise, to my joy and peace.

I remember, on one occasion, being away from home on a visit to friends, and being out for a walk very early one Sunday morning, when I heard the bells of a church chiming a tune, which I knew was sung to these words:

"We love the place, O God,
Wherein Thine honour dwells;
The joy of Thine abode,
All earthly joy excels."

I remember the sweetness which accompanied the words as they sprang up in my mind, and how it seemed to be an earnest of the good day I spent in God's house that Sunday. I heard a sermon from: "He knoweth the way that I take: *when* He hath tried me, I shall come forth as gold," and another from: "Make straight paths for your feet." This was at the "Old Baptist" Chapel, Devizes, and proved a time of refreshing.

Another help about this time was when I was searching the Bible for consolation, feeling very tried, and tossed to and fro. I lighted on Romans 1. 6., "Among whom are ye also the called of Jesus Christ," which again encouraged me to hope I was in the right way. One mark I knew I possessed – the love of the brethren. I felt it a sacred pleasure to listen to those who could tell of things done in the way, and delighted to hear two or three of the old people speak of their early days, and of the faithful ministers they used to hear, who were only names to me. I believe I was on the right side of that word: "We know that we have passed from death unto life, because we love the brethren," and I often left their company with the feeling:

"With them numbered may I be
Now, and in eternity."

I had regularly attended "Zion" Chapel, Wantage, from the time my eyes were opened, as there was a pastor there, also a Sunday School, and a Bible Class which I attended.

At length, when I had become much tried and tempted as to whether I was right for eternity, or no, I was brought very low, and I recall some of the solemn exercises of those days. All other matters were nothing, compared with this – heaven or hell? Which was I bound for? I did want it cleared up to my soul's happiness.

One Sunday morning, (after a time of wrestling prayer) I went up to the house of prayer feeling a solemn awe upon my mind, and almost like a man expecting to hear his sentence. As I write, I remember the feeling well, and how I looked for the subject to be announced, having such an expectation that the text would confirm the good work begun within, if indeed that blessed work was begun. Such were my exercises, and such the hope within my breast that God would speak to me, that, if the subject had been against me, and the preacher's commission had been given that day to pull down, and not to build up, I should have questioned the whole of God's dealings with me. I should have been ready to conclude I was one of the foolish virgins, having a lamp – a name to live – but no oil, no religion that God was the author of. My expectation proved to be well grounded. To my joy and peace, the subject was announced – "And ye are complete in Him" Colossians 2. 10. This word took fast hold of me, and was a nail fastened in a sure place. I felt it was God's Word to me, and I rejoiced therein. I had solemnly realized, that: "by the works of the law shall no flesh be justified," and had proved my own righteousness to be as filthy rags. I felt:

> "If ever my poor soul be saved,
> 'Tis Christ must be the way"

and now I felt I was *in* the way, having God's testimony for it.

I have often looked back to this time in the dealings of God with me, and have many times longed to feel as I did then. For a while the world seemed another place altogether, and I used to go out into the fields after working hours, and *all* nature seemed to me

> "To spread her Maker's praise abroad".

I felt such nearness to His throne, that I 'opened my mouth wide,' and asked for many things I felt laid on my mind at that time. Some of my prayers God answered in later years, by "terrible things in righteousness." I used to feel, at that time, that truly the Bible was the *Holy* Bible, and I found a sacred pleasure in searching its pages which I have, often since, longed to enjoy. Round about this time, my health began to fail, and I began to reap some of the consequences of the life I had pursued among the ungodly. This brought new exercises of mind, and I had to join with Moses: "If I have found grace in Thy sight, shew me now Thy way."

I was brought into a concern about making a public profession, and being baptized, and after much exercise of mind, I ventured forward. I knew from, The Acts of the Apostles, the right way into Church fellowship was through baptism by immersion, but I felt a solemn desire to be led aright therein. I was encouraged to feel I was the character referred to in Acts 2. 41. – "Then they that gladly received His Word were baptized:" for I knew I had been enabled to receive both the written and the incarnate Word, gladly. In my youth, my attitude was: "We will not have this *Man* to reign over us," but now I felt it was my soul's earnest desire that Jesus Christ should reign on the throne of my spiritual affections, and govern me and mine. I often would plead, in Kent's words:

> "Indulgent God, how kind
> Are all Thy ways to me,
> Whose dark benighted mind
> Was enmity with Thee;
> Yet, now, subdued by sovereign grace,
> My spirit longs for Thy embrace!"

One thing I thought to be against me was my youth (I was just turned 19 years of age), but I was brought to a decision, after much exercise, by considering that, as God had made me to differ from the world at large, it became me to make the difference as manifest as possible, and to publicly own the Lord Jesus. My former companions in sin knew how I had run in the ways of ungodliness with them, and I felt a solemn desire to bear witness that I was on the Lord's side. I wanted to enter into the psalmist's words: "I *am* a companion of all *them* that fear Thee" – I knew I could travel thus far, but I wanted to enter into the other half of the text – "and of them that keep Thy precepts." I knew one of the precepts was obedience to God's commands, and I gave in my name one Sunday evening, after a service wherein I had felt helped. I was tried about the matter while waiting the time appointed for the Church Meeting, but, on the day appointed, while at my work, my mind was sweetly confirmed that the thing was of the Lord, by the lines coming powerfully:

> "The soul that with sincere desires
> Seeks after Jesus' love,
> That soul the Holy Ghost inspires
> With breathings from above."

I was unanimously received by the Church, and was baptized on the 30th September, 1909.

As I look back upon this time, I can only liken my subsequent experience as faintly resembling that of the Lord Jesus, who, after He was baptized, was led into the wilderness. Truly, after a short while, I came into a wilderness experience. I cannot go into details, as it would not be profitable, but it will be enough to state that trouble arose in the Cause through the pastor being entangled and snared by the evil one, so that the world rejoiced, while the hearts of God's people were made sad thereby. (I fully believe he was a good man, and a useful minister, and he was brought to repentance, and eventually made a good end.) Alas, what havoc it wrought in our Cause. The hand of God seemed to go out against it, and whole families (and some of them large, and practically grown up) were removed in providence, and the Cause was brought low. The pastor resigned, and moved away, and only a few were left to carry on, and live down the reproach. As I was hardly 20 years old when this happened, it will be understood what a painful path it was to tread. I remember the tossings to and fro of those days, and the burden that was brought upon my spirit, and it was a long while ere I recovered from the effects of this Church trouble. I was the last one baptized by the pastor there, and none have gone down into the baptistery since. (The chapel was closed a few years afterwards, and ultimately sold, and later, much to the distress of the godly, became a Roman Catholic church, and, where God's servants used to preach the everlasting gospel, and proclaim Jesus Christ in His unsearchable riches, the abomination of the Romish Mass was celebrated. Where the Sun of Righteousness was wont to shine with His gladdening beams, cheering the mourners in Zion, there were found lighted candles upon a popish alter.)

As I was out of my apprenticeship, and desired to advance in my trade as a printer, I earnestly sought the Lord's leading. My mind was strongly impressed with a desire to labour in the printing works where, in 1910, the *Gospel Standard* was printed. I felt I should like to be engaged where, day by day, good books and godly men's lives, and other profitable literature was printed. God was graciously pleased to grant my request, and the way was opened, and I removed to Croydon.

It was not long before I found out West Street chapel, and became a regular worshipper there. I passed through many trying times at Croydon, as I was often overtaken by ill health, and hardly ever reflect on those days without thinking of Jeremiah's words: "Remembering mine affliction and my misery, the wormwood and the gall." I was in earnest to progress at my trade, and yet was not allowed to go forward, having one set-back after another. After being at West Street Chapel a while, the pastor asked me to transfer my membership to that Church, and feeling it to be a right step, I did so.

I was helped along with no outstanding waymarks to speak of, but, as the time went on, I got into a backsliding state. After two or three years struggling against ill health, I contracted a form of lead poisoning. One doctor after another declared I must give up the printing trade, but my heart was so wrapped up in it, that I rebelled against the prospect, as it would mean I should have to start life over again. My employers showed me kindness, and stood by me, but I had, at length, to give in. I remember on one occasion, when laid aside again, and feeling rebellious, and filled with self-pity, I was trying to plead with the Lord: "Why is this, Lord, why am I afflicted thus?" The answer came: "The way of transgressors *is* hard." I had to plead guilty that I was a transgressor in thought, word and deed, and put my mouth in the dust, and beg for mercy, and that I might be reconciled to God in His dealings with me. From this time, I began to see more that I was in the Lord's hands, for Him to mould my life as He saw fit, and my pleasant picture of, one day, owning and working a small printing office of my own, was marred.

My mind was made submissive and meekened while I was, one day, reading about Elijah by the brook Cherith, and as I came to the words: "And it came to pass after a while, that the brook dried up," so I was brought to feel concerning the dealings of God with me. I felt assured that Elijah's God would remember me, and that He would make His goodness pass before me in the way, and so He did.

My concern *now*, was to know what the mind of God was concerning me. Was I to remain where I was and seek fresh employment, or which way was I to take? I wanted to see the cloud move, and my prayer was:

"Guide me, O Thou great Jehovah!"

and, in a marked way, the Lord directed me. As I was thus concerned which way to take, the late Mr. John Booth came to supply at West Street chapel, and I felt particularly anxious that God would make him His messenger to me. I was a stranger to him, and I hoped I might hear a word in season. My exercise was, that God would give him a text that should be, in itself, a message to me. I felt my prayer was answered when he announced as his text, Luke 8. 39, "Return to thine own house, and shew how great things God hath done unto thee." Such was the force of this word, that I was enabled to act on it, and I returned home to my father and mother, there to watch the Lord's hand concerning the future.

As soon as I returned home to Wantage, I think almost the first Sunday following, when I went to "Zion" Chapel, the deacon asked me to take the service, and speak, if I felt led, to the people. A few still gathered there, and some of them loved the Truth, but the Cause was very low. I did not feel I could venture to speak to the people, as the deacon requested, feeling it to be a solemn matter, and also realizing my own need of teaching, yet I felt a willingness and a desire, *if God made the way*, to be a help in keeping open the doors of our poor afflicted "Zion". In the next chapter I will relate, as I am helped, how I was led to preach the gospel, beginning in this same "Zion" Chapel, Wantage.

Chapter 2

CALL TO THE MINISTRY

I feel the solemnity of attempting to pen an outline of what I hope are the dealings of God with me in connection with the work of the ministry. I believe the call to the ministry is distinct from one's call by grace, and that no work that mortals can be engaged in can compare with it. What greater honour can be known than to be used and owned of God in proclaiming the unsearchable riches of Christ, to the benefit and blessing of God's people, and His own glory?

When I first began to be concerned about standing up in God's name, I felt a solemn sense of my unfitness for a work of such solemnity and importance, and I realized, also, that a "Thus saith the Lord" was needful to evidence a divine commission. I had a view, at times, of the low state of some of our Causes and, in reading or hearing of this, I felt my mind stirred within me. Sometimes I felt burdened with exercises concerning the work, and then, at other times, I realized my youth, my unfitness and ignorance, and the solemn obligations of the minister's office, and sought to flee from the prospect of it; but the matter soon became uppermost in my mind again.

The first encouragement I received, to cause me to feel the Lord's hand was in the matter, was when I was pleading for some confirmation from Him that He was leading me, and that He would make the way plain for me to go, in His own time and way. The promise was: "Fear thou not; for I *am* with thee; be not dismayed; for I *am* thy God: I will strengthen thee; yea, I will help thee; yea, I will uphold thee with the right hand of My righteousness." Isaiah 41. 10. This word came early one morning as I was preparing to go to my work and, while it seemed too good to be true, I treasured it up, and have blessedly proved it to be true, and I still have to plead concerning it: "Remember the word unto Thy servant, upon which Thou hast caused me to hope." From this time of help, I began to watch the Lord's hand concerning the

163

matter.

I should say, also, that, taking an active interest in the Sunday School connected with our Cause at Tamworth Road, Croydon, I was called upon, on two or three occasions, to give addresses to the children gathered together there, and felt helped to do so. I learned in later years, to my surprise, that one or two of the older friends were impressed that God was leading me forth into the ministry. I know I felt it to be a solemn business, even to address the young, and the exercise connected therewith, brought me very low.

I was very much interested in Protestant work about this time, and laboured with my pen therein, but, as the Lord was pleased to give me a clearer insight into the word "Protestant", I was brought to see and feel that much of the work done by many Protestant Societies would not stand the fire. While they professed to have the One Foundation as their basis, much that was built thereon, being only a political or historical Protestantism, and some nought but free-will teaching (under a Calvinistic name) was but wood, hay, and stubble. As this matter was made plain to me, I ceased this work, and was brought to contend for an experimental knowledge of the Truth as the surest mark of being a true Protestant. I was earnest in my desires to labour in the Protestant cause, but I have lived long enough to prove a fuller meaning of Zechariah 4. 6: "Not by might, nor by power, but by My Spirit, saith the LORD of hosts."

I look back upon one waymark that I was helped to set up when recovering from an illness at Croydon, that I have never wholly lost sight of. I was walking along a street at West Croydon, when I met an old member of "Providence" Chapel, West Street, whose prayers and conversation were often profitable and edifying. To my surprise, after kindly greeting me, he began to enquire if I was a subject of exercises concerning the ministry, as the matter was much upon his mind. I felt that, as he was a grey-headed pilgrim, I could not refrain from answering, and told him that I was concerned about it. In the course of our conversation, my friend related how he had been led out in prayer on my behalf, and it was impressed upon his mind that some of the dealings of God with me were to fit me for the ministry. I remember well the solemn import of our conversation, and the weight that attended the words that my friend spoke. One thing that took hold of me was an apt remark concerning Joseph and his dreams; and he told me, if God designed me to stand up in His name, I must expect to be tried and tempted, and to go through the fire, if I was to be made a good minister of Jesus Christ.

I went on my way thinking about my friend's words, especially one which he quoted during our conversation: "Until the time that His Word came: the Word of the LORD tried him." This word continued with me all day until, at length, in going to the week evening service, I felt constrained to desire that, if the Lord's hand was in the matter, and that my friend was rightly led in his feeling towards me, He would lead the pastor, Mr. W. Brooke, to preach from it, and that should be a token for good. My mind was on the stretch during the earlier part of the service, especially as the chapter read was upon Joseph's trials. To my encouragement, Mr. Brooke announced his text: Psalm 105. 19, "Until the time that His word came: the Word of the LORD tried him," and he touched upon many things that fitted in with our morning conversation. I found my friend, after the service, was quite overcome by the clinching of our conversation by the evening subject, and although he did not live to hear me preach, he was confirmed in his feeling toward me.

Following on this, the late Mr. S. Curtis very kindly invited me to spend a time at his house at Southill, in the hope that the change might benefit my health. I found it to be as an oasis in a desert, to be under the roof of the Chapel House, Southill, and I shall never forget the kindness shown me by my friends there. I received much good counsel from God's dear servant, and he seemed to enter into my exercises, and sympathize with me, and to encourage me to watch the Lord's hand. At that time, there were three services each Sunday at Southill, Mr. Curtis preaching morning and afternoon, and, in the evening, a Prayer Meeting was held, when an address was given, (Mr. Curtis usually being engaged at neighbouring Causes on Sunday evenings). On the first Sunday I was there, to my surprise, Mr. Curtis asked me if I would try to give an address at the evening service, as it was on his mind to ask me to do so. As there were usually young people present at the evening service, and knowing I had given two or three addresses at Tamworth Road Sunday School, and feeling the hand of the Lord was in it, I promised, as He should help me, to do so. I hope the Lord did help me, and also on the two following Sunday evenings, which confirmed me that my exercises were of the Lord, and that, in His time, I should see the door more widely opened.

On my return to my home in Wantage, I continued to seek the Lord concerning the way being made plain, and, at length, I obtained the token for good I needed. I had felt an unusual freedom in seeking the Lord in this matter, especially as I walked around the fields near my home and, on one or two occasions, in my father's greenhouse. One Saturday evening, I went out for a walk, and met an old friend who had left Wantage some years before, but who used to be a deacon of "Zion" Chapel and also Sunday School superintendent; I believe it was of the Lord that we should meet. I had not the slightest thought he was in our neighbourhood, and I could but view the hand of God in our meeting thus, as we had not been long in conversation upon the things of God ere he began to speak to me upon the work of the ministry, and his thoughts concerning me therein. I felt my mind opened to speak of some of the exercises I was the subject of, and for well-nigh two hours we remained by a stile in a field, going into the things connected with the work of the ministry, and the right way to enter upon it. I told my friend I was earnestly hoping I should get some light upon the matter the following day at Grove chapel, when Mr. W. West, of Heathfield, was expected to preach. My mind seemed solemnly impressed that God would give His servant a message for me, as I had felt such encouragement at the Throne of Grace in pleading for it. (At this time there were only Sunday evening services at "Zion" Chapel, Wantage.)

On the Sunday morning, I went to God's house and was much

tried as to whether my desires would be granted. There were very few in the congregation, but I lost sight of this when Mr. West stood up and announced his chapter to read (Isaiah 62) and began: "For Zion's sake will I not hold my peace," and so the dear man read on. How the words seemed to fit in: "I have set watchmen upon thy walls, O Jerusalem, *which* shall never hold their peace day nor night: ye that make mention of the LORD, keep not silence." When Mr. West read the tenth verse, which sets forth a minister's commission to preach the gospel, I lifted up my heart and asked the Lord that His servant might take that for his subject, and then I should indeed know that it was right for me to stand upon Zion's walls to preach the gospel, as He enabled me. When the prayer was ended, the clerk announced Hymn 329, and said: "We will begin at the third verse":

"Fear not, I am with thee; O be not dismayed;
I, I am thy God, and will still give thee aid;
I'll strengthen thee, help thee, and cause thee to stand,
Upheld by My righteous, omnipotent hand."

This brought back the first promise laid upon my mind, as before related (Isaiah 41. 10), "Fear thou not, for I *am* with thee: be not dismayed; for I *am* thy God: I will strengthen thee; yea, I will help thee; yea I will uphold thee with the right hand of My righteousness." I felt it was the Lord's doings, and when dear Mr. West stood up, before he announced his text, he said: "Friends, I have had to come all the way from Heathfield to Grove to speak about the work of the ministry, and how God thrusts a man into it. You will find my text in Isaiah 62. 10. 'Go through, go through the gates; prepare ye the way of the people; cast up, cast up the highway; gather out the stones; lift up a standard for the people.'"

He was helped to open this up in such a way that I felt I must no longer hold back, but go wherever a door was opened. My friend, who had been with me the previous evening, was a hearer also; and could not but be confirmed in his impressions concerning me, and was persuaded the thing was from the Lord. This friend was long a living witness of that memorable Sunday morning's service, and later became my father-in-law (although, at that time, there was not the slightest likelihood of such a relationship between us).

I now felt I could help at "Zion" Chapel, Wantage, which was being carried on by the few who remained there, and, although I had said "No!" to the deacon's repeated invitations to preach there, when he asked me again if I would do so on Sunday evening, 12th July, I promised, as the Lord should help me, to do so. This was shortly after hearing Mr. West at Grove. I was much concerned on that Sunday evening, and could truly say: "I was with you in weakness, and in fear, and in much trembling," but I was helped to preach from Isaiah 24. 15. – "Wherefore glorify ye the LORD in the fires." I continued to preach at "Zion" Chapel when there was no other minister engaged, and not without some encouragement.

After a while, I was tried as to whether I was sent to preach or no, and the evil one filled my mind with suggestions that, if I *was* sent to preach, God would open doors elsewhere, and make it manifest that He had a work for me to do. This brought about further exercise of mind that the Lord would go before me and open doors, and thus establish my call to the ministry. I soon received a very kind letter from the deacon of our Cause at Hook Norton, Oxon., asking me to preach there on 23rd August, 1914. Following this, came other invitations to Causes in Bucks., Herts., and Kent, and then Wilts., and some of them where *all* were strangers to me. I found it encouraging to watch the Lord's hand in how doors were opened.

For instance, I found that I received an invitation to a Cause in Bucks., through another minister, who had heard me give an address, months before, in London, and felt, at the time, the Lord was leading me into the ministry. He spoke of his thoughts concerning me to a deacon of a Cause where he was supplying, who felt his mind led to send me an invitation to preach, which came at a time when I was pleading for further confirmation concerning my call.

I remember the burdened state I was in, not only regarding the ministry, but my circumstances, and weak state of health, and my felt unfitness, all the week previous to my first journey away to preach at Hook Norton. I had to plead with the Lord that, if He had arranged my engagement to preach there, would He send me the means to undertake the journey. I was living under my parents' roof, who were very kind to me, but, as they were poor, I felt this matter was one between God and my own soul. On the Saturday morning I was due to set out on my journey, a letter came from a friend encouraging me, and containing a Postal Order for just the amount needed for my journey to Hook Norton. So I went forth with a hope the hand of God was overruling it, and, to His honour, I would speak that I believe it was in accord with His eternal purposes I should preach at "Zion" Chapel, Hook Norton, on that day. I was helped through the day's services there, receiving a most kind welcome, and was encouraged by the friends' testimony of having heard to profit. In later days, I found that, on that day, God gave me a seal to my ministry, and some years after, that candidate was the first I had the pleasure to baptize.

From this time onward, I continued to go wherever doors were opened, often labouring amidst many discouragements and set-backs, and the sense of the great importance of the work, and my great unfitness to be engaged in it. And, I may add that this pathway is the same I travel now, but, as I look back over it, and review it, I should not honour the Lord if I left the statement there. I can also say, that, when I have realized God's presence in preaching the gospel, and found His Word made a blessing to the hearers, I have felt ready and willing to travel in any way God saw fit to lead me in, if He would but make my ministry a blessing indeed, and give me all needed grace to stand on Zion's walls to His own glory, and to the good of His dear people.

"Union" Chapel Bethersden
as it was during Mr Dawson's pastorate

Chapter 3

CALL TO THE PASTORATE AT "UNION" CHAPEL, BETHERSDEN

In my early days at "Union" Chapel, there were questions arising about the standing of our Cause, owing to my predecessor being an editor of the *Earthen Vessel* magazine. I feel a desire to show how the matter stood when I came, and how the Cause stands now. I would state, first of all, that having only a knowledge of "Gospel Standard" Causes, I knew nothing of the difference between the two denominations until the year I commenced to preach. I went to a service, at a friend's request, in an "Earthen Vessel" Cause, and heard the pastor at a week-evening service. I could tell there was a difference, not only in the style of service, but also in one's feelings as a worshipper, as there did not seem to be the same atmosphere. (I desire to mention, that later on in my ministerial life, I gathered there were many in such Causes, who were desirous to worship God aright, who knew little or nothing of the grievous error of doctrine which, a hundred years ago, brought about such a cleavage in our denominational life. Nothwithstanding their environment, they were taught of God to believe that Jesus Christ was the Eternal Son of God in His divine nature, and not the Son of God by office, and, on that sure foundation, their hope of heaven was built.)

From this time I began to realize there were more sorts of Strict Baptists than one, and I felt a firm persuasion that I wanted to remain among those people often referred to as "Standard" people.

When I was first invited to preach at "Union" Chapel, Bethersden, I knew nothing whatever of the place or people. I had once journeyed through Kent on my way to spend a short holiday at Folkestone, and I little thought, as I looked out of the train when passing through Pluckley Station, that a little way off was a sphere of labour God designed me to fill.

I have often pondered how the purposes of God hinge upon what seem, at the time, to be little incidents in life's journey. So it was, in my coming to Bethersden. I called in the offices of a well-known Protestant society in London one afternoon in the year 1914, and while there, I was introduced to the deacon of "Union" Chapel, who also had called to see the secretary, who was a personal friend of his. Learning from the secretary that I had begun to preach among our Causes, he asked me if I would supply on a vacant Sunday at Bethersden, 22nd November, 1914. After prayerful consideration, I felt my mind free to do so.

As I journeyed from my Berkshire home to Bethersden at the appointed time to fulfil my engagement, I had a solemn feeling there was some deep underlying purpose to my visit. I was given a very kind welcome where I was entertained, and on the Sunday morning I stood up, in a chapel that seats 250 people, before a congregation of 16 grown-ups and about half-a-dozen children – so low had the Cause become. The later congregations were larger, and I felt helped in preaching, but it was more pulling down than building up. I was asked to give some more Sundays in the ensuing year, and I felt constrained to do so; the first of these was 3rd January, 1915.

I little thought when I set out on the Saturday morning, 2nd January, from Berkshire, for four or five days in Kent, that it would be the end of April before I reached home again, but so it worked out. I felt very unwell while I was fulfilling my engagement at "Union" Chapel, and after preaching on the Wednesday evening from 1 Corinthians 14. 8. ("For if the trumpet give an uncertain sound, who shall prepare himself to the battle?") I was taken seriously ill. A large ulcer developed in my stomach, and I laid at death's door for a day or two, and then my illness took a turn for the better, but it was some weeks ere I recovered enough to go out to God's house. On Sunday afternoon, 21st February, I preached again at "Union" Chapel from Psalm 11. 5. ("The LORD trieth the righteous").
Three things stood out in this affliction.

(i) The goodness of God in going before me in laying me aside under the roof of a godly widow, who, having profited under my ministry, felt her heart moved to do all she could on my behalf. And the kindness I received at her hands I shall never forget, as she defrayed the whole of the expenses of my illness, giving me the large doctor's bill, receipted later on in the year. I have often admired the hand of God in arranging this for me, as, when I arrived at Bethersden, on that occasion, to preach, I had only a few coppers in my pocket. My illness was such that I needed special care in the early stages of it, and I received it. The name of the house where I was laid aside was "Ebenezer", and truly I set up some "Ebenezers" there.

(ii) In this affliction I was favoured, for a while, to rejoice in the Lord, and, realizing the spirit of adoption, was made to feel I possessed a heavenly Father, who knew all my needs, and enabled me to sing:

"My every need He richly will supply;
Nor will His mercy ever let me die.

(iii) As I was recovering from my illness, friends came to see me, and I began to get an insight into the troubles surrounding "Union" Chapel, and, as I listened to one and another, I was helped to ponder over matters, and I hope the Lord enabled me to act aright therein. I gathered that difficulties concerning the ministry had for some time been of such a nature that some who belonged to the Cause had gone to neighbouring Causes to worship, hence one of the causes of the low state of "Union" Chapel. As I regained strength, I was helped to preach on week evenings, and some Sundays, the congregations increasing, and there was a return of those who had formerly worshipped at the Cause.

From this time, a movement began among some of the people that I might be fixed as the pastor at Bethersden, and I believe some were much exercised about the matter, and felt a spirit of prayer concerning it. On the other hand, there were those whose hearts were not for it, as my ministry, at that time, was of a stripping nature, and they knew that my coming among them would lead to alterations in the carrying on of the Cause, which they did not wish to see brought about. As for me, I felt it would be like Jonah going to Nineveh, if I had to be fixed in such a sphere of labour. Before I left Bethersden in the last week of April, I was asked definitely to give all the engagements I could, (God willing) that the hand of God might be observed in the matter, and I felt my mind made up to do so.

The matters in connection with "Union" Chapel were not long out of my mind, even when I was engaged in preaching at other Causes, my thoughts would centre upon that Cause, and I had many searchings of heart as to what God's purposes were concerning it.

I would here say that my predecessor in the pastorate, some years before, was maintained practically by one liberal supporter of the Cause, who had passed away before I visited Bethersden. When I came, the Cause was carried on chiefly by the aid of the Strict and Particular Baptist Society, who sent ministers down for a number of Sundays. (Of this Society I knew nothing at that time.)

It was gradually felt, by most in connection with "Union" Chapel, that my coming among the people was ordered of God, as there were signs following the Word preached, and some within the Church were more established in the Truth. God had brought me back from the brink of the grave, and I felt led to contend, very solemnly, for a religion that would stand in a dying hour, and as I had been brought low in my illness ere I was lifted up, I contended for this in my ministry. I hope God was pleased to own my labours, so that, at length, a Church Meeting was called, and I was asked to take the oversight of the Cause. Some who at first opposed, not being able to gainsay the Lord's blessing that had attended my labours, and the signs of revival in the Cause, were made to 'be still' at the Church Meeting. While they did not vote for it, God would not allow them to vote against it. (Of the minority, some were soon laid in the grave, and one or two removed in providence.)

The matter being thus brought to a climax, and my mind still being unsettled, I still felt like Jonah when he was first sent to Nineveh. I could see some matters that would need to be straightened out ere one could truly feel the Cause was in order, and I wanted some ground to hope that, in God's time and way, the Cause might be revived and prosper.

My mind was made up, at length, to ask the Church to allow me to state at a Church Meeting what I considered must be attended to before I could arrive at a right decision regarding the pastorate. A Meeting was arranged, and I remember the solemn feelings I laboured under in attending it.

I made it plain that I should seek, as the Lord gave me grace, to carry on the Cause in accord with the doctrines in the Trust Deed (which I carefully examined), and pointed out that I was wholly in sympathy with the "Gospel Standard" line of things, as I had known no other.

To my amazement, all the matters I named were agreed to by a good majority, and thus the thing now laid between the Lord and my own conscience. I have to acknowledge I began to look to an arm of flesh, and did unwisely. I consulted with one or two friends who knew me and wished me well, and their advice was: "Have nothing to do with a Cause which has been known as a rather 'wide' Cause," and I became full of tossings to and fro as to how far such counsel could be right. My friend, Mr. John Kemp, pastor of "Ebenezer" Chapel, Biddenden, put his word in on the other side of the scale, and encouraged me, as he hoped the thing was of the Lord, having been much exercised about our Cause and its low estate.

At length, my mind was settled regarding *this* matter by these words being brought forcibly to my mind: "Then Philip went down to the city of *Samaria*, and preached Christ unto them" Acts

8. 5., and now I sought for a further answer from the Lord – I wanted the fleece wet and dry. I waited six or seven weeks, and obtained no light – no word; and, meanwhile, I had three or four heavy seasons in "Union" Chapel pulpit, and felt unwilling to become the pastor, feeling as I did. (I did not realize, at that time, I might be the "prisoner of the Lord," that some hearers, in bondage, might be set at liberty.)

One Monday morning, I laid awake (after a Sunday at "Union" Chapel when I felt shut up) and began to reason the matter out. I thought: "I have waited on the Lord and He has not bid me go, and, therefore, it means that it is not His will that I should become the pastor of this Cause." Meditating thus, my mind seemed to settle down, and I sat up in bed, to begin to dress, thinking I would write a refusal to the Church. As I sat up in bed, light sprang up in my breast, and this word seemed to stream into my heart: "Son, go work today in my vineyard. He answered and said, I will not: but afterward he repented, and went" Matthew 21. 28, 29. and so did I. Such a feeling came upon me – love to the Lord – His Cause and interest at Bethersden, submission to His will, and willingness to serve Him wherever He appointed, I shall never forget it. If an angel had come into my room then, and told me that I was to be burned in our village street for the Truth's sake, after preaching so many years as "Union" Chapel pastor, I should have said: "*I will go.*"

I rose from my bed with very different feelings from what at first possessed me, and, when I went downstairs, the Bible laid on the breakfast table in readiness for family worship. I sat down, and while waiting for my friends, I lifted up my heart, and begged one more confirming token for good, that it was the Lord's will I should accept the pastorate. I opened the Bible to look for a chapter to read, and the first word my eye lighted upon was Zechariah 8. 12: ("For the seed *shall be* prosperous; the vine shall give her fruit, and the ground shall give her increase, and the heavens shall give their dew; and I will cause the remnant of this people to possess all these *things*"). The words seemed to stand out in embossed letters on the page. This word clinched the matter, and, under the sweetness of the humbling I had received, I accepted the Church's invitation, and became the pastor of "Union" Chapel, Bethersden. My earnest prayer was in accord with the psalmist's words: "Return, we beseech Thee, O God of hosts: look down from heaven, and behold, and visit this vine; And the vineyard which Thy right hand hath planted, and the branch *that* Thou madest strong for Thyself" Psalm 80. 14-15., which subject I brought before the people on the Sunday my acceptance of the pastorate was announced publicly.

Our "Union" Chapel friends at the present time, may like to read copies of two letters I sent to the Church concerning the pastorate. The first letter is in reply to one from the Church asking if I would consider a call, if sent, and the second letter speaks for itself.

To the Church of Christ meeting for worship at "Union" Chapel, Bethersden.

Dear Friends,

I heartily reciprocate the kindly feelings expressed in your letter to me, and I desire to say that my earnest cry for you is that peace and prosperity may reign among you, and that it may be a good and pleasant sight to see the people who frequent "Union" Chapel all dwelling together in unity.

As regards the matters mentioned in your letter to me, relating to the important consideration of the pastorate of the Church, these must be left in the hands of the Lord, who makes no mistakes in such matters. Suffice it to say that, if the Church should honour me by giving me such an invitation, I should seek to lay the matter earnestly before the Throne of grace, and look to God alone for an answer. My thoughts are as the good man of ancient days expressed: "If Thy presence go not *with me*, carry us not up hence" Exodus 33. 15.

In such a solemn matter, I would earnestly ask you, as a Church, to wrestle and pray daily that God's hand may be plainly seen directing yourselves and me. May the Lord graciously help you to look away from man, not considering his abilities or gifts, but may He lead you to look to Him alone, who has chosen the foolish and ignorant of this world to preach the everlasting gospel, many times, and who puts to confusion the wisdom of this world, by those depending upon it, to do so.

It is right for Churches to seek pastors, and the promise is: "I will give you pastors according to mine heart" Jeremiah 3. 15. So my desire is that, if you have any thoughts regarding myself as being a likely man to be the pastor of "Union" Chapel, you will wrestle earnestly before the Lord that it may be seen *He* has given me to you to be the pastor of the Church. Such a pastorate would be prosperous; all else would be man's work, and not God's, consequently, it would fall to the ground, and be unfruitful; hence it is written: "Except the LORD build the house, they labour in vain that build it" Psalm 127. 1.

> With Christian greetings to you all,
> Yours in hope of salvation by grace,
> HERBERT DAWSON.

To the Church of Christ meeting for worship at "Union" Chapel, Bethersden.

Dear Friends,

After a lapse of many days, I have been able to come to a decision respecting the acceptance of the pastorate of "Union" Chapel. Many cries, and much exercise of mind, also the prayers of many friends, have at last enabled me to observe the fleece wet and dry also. Therefore I desire (as the Lord shall help me) to accept the invitation which you were pleased to extend to me.

What shall I say? Just this: "Who is sufficient for these things?" "Brethren, pray for us." Promises I shall not make, nor must you expect any great things, but it will be a mercy if we can hold on our way in peace, love and union. I do not believe in any sounding of trumpets or bombastic statements, so that I shall content myself by saying that, *as the Lord is graciously pleased to strengthen and uphold me* I shall "spend, and be spent", among you.

> "Go, labour on; spend, and be spent;
> My work to do the Master's will."

My prayer is that peace may reign in our Cause, and the sun of prosperity shine upon us.

Three things I would say, and they are these:

1. "Let no man despise thy (my) youth."
2. "Be of *one* mind, live in peace; and the God of love and peace shall be with you."
3. "Leave off contention before it be meddled with."
   "Where no wood is, *there* the fire goeth out: so where *there* is no talebearer, the strife ceaseth."

I hope the Spirit of Christ may be evident among us, enabling us to forgive, and be pitiful, and kind one to another. "Now if any man have not the Spirit of Christ, he is none of His." Let us love one another "in deed and in truth."

And now, dear friends, I commend you to God, and to the Word of His grace. "Let all bitterness, and wrath, and anger, and clamour, and evil speaking, be put away from you, with all malice; And be ye kind one to another, tenderhearted, forgiving one another, even as God for Christ's sake hath forgiven you."

May the Lord build us up as a people, strengthen me as your pastor, and enable us to exalt the Lord Jesus Christ, and abase ourselves. Thus might our union be to His honour and glory. Amen.

With Christian love, and a desire for your best welfare,
Yours in truth,
HERBERT DAWSON.
June, 1915.

(In this letter, some of the Scriptures quoted have special reference to the trials which had beset the Cause ere I came to "Union" Chapel.)

As the time went on, the few who wanted smooth things became fewer still; some going out from us because they were not of us, and others being carried to the churchyard. God was graciously pleased to gather in others, some of whom, with many of their children, and children's children, have continued with us until now. Many also have been well laid in the grave. I hope not a few among us possess an ear to hear, and do receive the Truth in the love of it. I have many times felt my own unfitness for the place I fill, and often long to enter into a more lively and gracious experience of the Truth I try to preach. I am fully persuaded that, unless a man preaches with the power of the Holy Ghost sent down from heaven, no Church, or Cause, can be rightly built up. Alas, this preaching is very scarce, according to one's feelings, often; and yet I feel also that, when a man is fixed by God in a particular sphere of labour, He will grant His blessed aid, and the grace and wisdom needed for that man to fill it to God's own honour and glory, and to bring about His eternal purposes.

I asked to be supported by voluntary contributions, believing this to be Scriptural, and also feeling the hand of God would be thus observed in confirming me in the pastorate. I humbly hope God has been pleased to do so. I can say: 'Goodness and mercy have followed me all the days of my life,' and during the years of my pastorate especially. My dear wife and I have many times looked on while the angel of the Lord has done wondrously for us in providence and in grace. Also, I must say the Lord has often favoured me to feel I am in my right place, by confirming the Word by signs following, during my pastorate. I can humbly declare: "Thou hast dealt well with Thy servant, O LORD."

I can best sum it all up in Paul's words: "Having therefore obtained help of God, I continue unto this day." My concern now is, to be helped to make full proof of my ministry, and endure to the end.

Chapter 4

"MY WIFE"
AN INDELIBLE MEMORY

In one of his Psalms of thanksgiving, David declares: "This *is* the day *which* the LORD has made; we will rejoice and be glad in it," referring to an outstanding day in Israel's history. Such a day, in which there was rejoicing in Israel, also leads our thoughts to the day when great David's greater Son came into the world to save sinners, and when He, though "despised and rejected of men," was manifested as the sure Foundation Stone upon which the Church is being built up, and against which the gates of hell cannot prevail.

There are days, outstanding in the lives of heaven-bound pilgrims, when it can feelingly be realized: *"This* is *the day* which *the LORD hath made*," and such a day in my life was 28th October, 1915. On that day, my dear wife and I were joined together by God at "Bethel" Chapel, St. Albans, Herts., and, for nearly fifty years, we have journeyed on through life together, walking in sweet agreement in the things of God, which wonderfully confirms us our Wedding Day was one the Lord indeed had made. I cannot put into words all that the Lord has made her to me, in my life as "Union" Chapel pastor, but she has shared my sorrows and joys, and by her loving fellowship, encouraged me in my labours. Often I have prized her counsel, and, in all my engagements to preach, whether at home or elsewhere, I have been strengthened by the remembrance of how I lived in her prayers for me, that I might ever be the "LORD's messenger in the LORD's message" upon Zion's walls. My wife has had many a reminder: "we must through much tribulation enter into the kingdom of God," as, for many years, she has been physically handicapped with heart trouble; but, many times, she has blessedly proved: "Out of weakness were made strong," and could confess:

> "For though our cup seems filled with gall,
> There's something secret sweetens all."

Herbert and Elsie Dawson
circa 1965

The lot of a pastor's wife is often a difficult one, inasmuch as, when her husband is away from home, (serving other Churches), a greater responsibility rests upon her in the family circle, especially when the children are growing up. In this aspect of the life of a pastor's wife, my own dear wife has been helped wonderfully, and found grace to help in time of need, and wisdom from above to handle complicated matters, wisely. I have often admired how frequently she has been kept in an exercised frame of mind, realizing *her need of Divine aid*, and that aid has been given. I desire, ever to thank God in the remembrance of all that, by His grace, she has been made to me and mine, and how she lives in the love and esteem of our "Union" Chapel people.

I include in this memory a copy of some verses I much prize, which I found awaiting me on my desk in the early days of our married life.

MY WISH

I would not ask for you, my love,
Riches, or honour, name or fame;
But rather pray that you may prove –
Comfort, when you God's Truth proclaim;
That, while you break the gospel bread,
Your soul may be most richly fed;

That while you speak of Jesus' worth,
His love, His glory, and His grace;
The merits of His blood set forth,
And beauty in the Saviour trace;
You may, by faith, most sweetly view
Your interest in salvation too.

When with rich promises divine
You strive the downcast soul to cheer,
Then may the Holy Spirit shine,
And *you* the warmth and radiance share;
That *you*, who tend with care the roots,
May be partaker of the fruits.

When you would show to God's dear saints
That treasured up in Jesus lies –
Strength, grace, redress for all complaints,
Pardon for all iniquities;
O, may *you* then most clearly view
That fullness dwells in Him for *you*;

So the sweet truths of sovereign grace,
Which now you preach from day to day,
Will cheer, while you the desert trace,
And be *your* solace, and *your* stay;
Till in heaven's nobler song *you* swell
It's notes divine – its praises tell.

Elsie J. Dawson.

"Blessed *be* the LORD, that hath given rest unto His people Israel, according to all that He promised: there hath not failed one word of all His good promise, which He promised by the hand of Moses His servant. The LORD our God be with us, as He was with our fathers: let Him not leave us, nor forsake us:" 1 Kings 8. 56, 57.

"OUR HOPE FOR YEARS TO COME"

*"Commit thy way unto the LORD; trust also in
Him; and He shall bring* it *to pass" – Psalm 37. 5.*

Tell God thy many wants and fears;
Tell Him the cause of all thy tears;
Tell Him the burdens that oppress,
For He alone can truly bless.

Commit thy way unto the Lord,
And ask for faith to trust His Word;
For He will surely bring to pass
That which for thee He purposes.

Commit thy way, though ills you dread,
And darkness veils the path you tread;
Stay on the name of Christ thy Lord,
For He is faithful to His Word.

And He has said to such as thee –
 "In all thy ways acknowledge Me";
I will direct thy paths, and thou
Shalt in a way of safety go.

Commit to Him thy heart's desire, –
That secret thing which, as a fire,
Burns in thy bones, nor gives thee rest; –
Leave that with Him; He knows the best.

Commit thy way, though He should seem
To hear thee not, and thou esteem
Thyself too vile, and e'en thy prayer
Too sinful for the Lord to hear.

Commit thy way, nor fear to tread
The path where He Himself doth lead;
However dark and rough the way,
The Lord will be thy strength and stay.

Commit thy way to Him, and prove
Jehovah's faithfulness and love;
For till life's close He then will be
A Guide and Counsellor to thee.

Elsie Dawson.
1915.

GRACE ALL-SUFFICIENT

"And God is able to make all grace abound toward YOU" 2 Cor. 9. 8.

"My grace is sufficient for thee"
    The promise I know and believe;
But I long from my fears to be free,
    And life-giving grace to receive.

I am pained with the burden of sin;
    My failings and faults I deplore;
I am troubled without and within,
    And long for free grace to restore.

O why should I comfortless be,
    And why for my want of grace grieve?
My ruin and poverty see,
    And long for the Lord to relieve?

Can it be there is no grace for me -
    No water in Bethlehem's well?
Yet I read: - "Grace sufficient for THEE"; -
    And why not for me? - Who can tell?

I'll wait on the God of all grace,
    Who can give me all grace, rich and free;
At His feet I will lay my sad case, -
    I shall find grace sufficient for ME.

Herbert Dawson

Memorial stone in Bethersden Parish graveyard

OTHER TITLES AVAILABLE

Tell It To The Generation Following (J.E.Pack)
An interesting book that traces the grace of God manifested in the lives
of several members of the Pack family through four generations.

Unanswered Prayer (G.D.Buss)
The author seeks to address some of the difficulties that the trial of faith
poses when the prayers of some believers may appear to go unanswered.

The King's Daughters (B.A.Ramsbottom)
The lives of 16 godly women who all bore testimony to the power of
God's grace.

Servant of a Covenant God (J.R.Broome)
The remarkable life and times of John Warburton who for many years
was pastor of Zion chapel Trowbridge.

Six Remarkable Ministers (B.A.Ramsbottom)
A most interesting account of how 6 very different men were raised up
by God to become ministers of the gospel.

Gadsby's Hymnbook
Contains over 1100 hymns composed by Gadsby, Wesley, Watts,
Newton, Hart, Steele, Cennick, Berridge, Cowper, Toplady and others.

Magazines
The *Gospel Standard* magazine was founded in 1835 and is essentially a
spiritual magazine that contends earnestly for the doctrines of free and
sovereign grace.
The *Friendly Companion* was founded in 1875 and is aimed at children
and young people.

Full book list obtainable from:
Gospel Standard Trust Publications
12(b) Roundwood Lane
Harpenden
Herts
AL5 3DD
England